AZERBAIJAN

Seven Years of Conflict in Nagorno-Karabakh

Human Rights Watch/Helsinki

Human Rights Watch
New York • Washington • Los Angeles • London • Brussels

Library of Congress Catalog Card Number: 94-79484
ISBN 1-56432-142-8

Cover photographs:
On the right: Azeri dead from fighting in Karabakh buried in "Martyr's Cemetery," Baku. Located high above the Caspian on a bluff, it used to be Kirov Park, Baku's loveliest, named in honor of the Bolshevik revolutionary.
On the left: Karabakh Armenian dead buried in main cemetery, Stepanakert, Nagorno-Karabakh.

HUMAN RIGHTS WATCH

Human Rights Watch conducts regular, systematic investigations of human rights abuses in some seventy countries around the world. It addresses the human rights practices of governments of all political stripes, of all geopolitical alignments, and of all ethnic and religious persuasions. In internal wars it documents violations by both governments and rebel groups. Human Rights Watch defends freedom of thought and expression, due process and equal protection of the law; it documents and denounces murders, disappearances, torture, arbitrary imprisonment, exile, censorship and other abuses of internationally recognized human rights.

Human Rights Watch began in 1978 with the founding of its Helsinki division. Today, it includes five divisions covering Africa, the Americas, Asia, the Middle East, as well as the signatories of the Helsinki accords. It also includes five collaborative projects on arms transfers, children's rights, free expression, prison conditions, and women's rights. It maintains offices in New York, Washington, Los Angeles, London, Brussels, Moscow, Belgrade, Zagreb, Dushanbe, and Hong Kong. Human Rights Watch is an independent, nongovernmental organization, supported by contributions from private individuals and foundations worldwide. It accepts no government funds, directly or indirectly.

The staff includes Kenneth Roth, executive director; Cynthia Brown, program director; Holly J. Burkhalter, advocacy director; Ann Johnson, development director; Gara LaMarche, associate director; Juan Méndez, general counsel; Susan Osnos, communications director; and Derrick Wong, finance and administration director.

The regional directors of Human Rights Watch are Abdullahi An-Na'im, Africa; José Miguel Vivanco, Americas; Sidney Jones, Asia; Jeri Laber, Helsinki; and Christopher E. George, Middle East. The project directors are Joost R. Hiltermann, Arms Project; Lois Whitman, Children's Rights Project; Gara LaMarche, Free Expression Project; and Dorothy Q. Thomas, Women's Rights Project.

The members of the board of directors are Robert L. Bernstein, chair; Adrian W. DeWind, vice chair; Roland Algrant, Lisa Anderson, Peter D. Bell, Alice L. Brown, William Carmichael, Dorothy Cullman, Irene Diamond, Edith Everett, Jonathan Fanton, Alan Finberg, Jack Greenberg, Alice H. Henkin, Harold Hongju Koh, Stephen L. Kass, Marina Pinto Kaufman, Alexander MacGregor, Josh Mailman, Peter Osnos, Kathleen Peratis, Bruce Rabb, Orville Schell, Gary G. Sick, Malcolm Smith, Nahid Toubia, Maureen White, and Rosalind C. Whitehead.

Addresses for Human Rights Watch
485 Fifth Avenue, New York, NY 10017-6104
Tel: (212) 972-8400, Fax: (212) 972-0905, E-mail: hrwnyc@hrw.org

1522 K Street, N.W., #910, Washington, DC 20005-1202
Tel: (202) 371-6592, Fax: (202) 371-0124, E-mail: hrwdc@hrw.org

10951 West Pico Blvd., #203, Los Angeles, CA 90064-2126
Tel: (310) 475-3070, Fax: (310) 475-5613, E-mail: hrwatchla@igc.apc.org

33 Islington High Street, N1 9LH London, UK
Tel: (71) 713-1995, Fax: (71) 713-1800, E-mail: hrwatchuk@gn.apc.org

15 Rue Van Campenhout, 1040 Brussels, Belgium
Tel: (2) 732-2009, Fax: (2) 732-0471, E-mail: hrwatcheu@gn.apc.org

ACKNOWLEDGMENTS

This report is based on a mission to Azerbaijan, Armenia, and the Nagorno-Karabakh Autonomous Oblast conducted by Human Rights Watch/Helsinki researchers[1] in March and April, 1994. Christopher Panico, Human Rights Watch/Helsinki researcher, Jemera Rone, Human Rights Watch Counsel, and Fatemah Ziai, Human Rights Watch/Helsinki researcher, visited Azerbaijan from March 23 to April 6, 1994, including the capital Baku, and the cities of Gobustan, Saatli, Sabirabad, Yevlakh, Barda, and Agjabedi. From April 8 to April 21, 1994, Christopher Panico and Alexander Petrov, Human Rights Watch/Helsinki researcher, visited Yerevan, Armenia, and Nagorno-Karabakh. During their five-day stay in Karabakh, they visited the towns of Stepanakert,[2] Askeran, Shusha, Krasnyi Bazar, and traveled to Fizuli in occupied Azerbaijan.

They spoke with refugees, displaced persons, government officials, journalists, human rights activists, foreign embassies, international aid organizations, prisoners of war, and hostages and their families.

Christopher Panico wrote the report; Jemera Rone edited it and also wrote the legal section. Rachel Denber proofread the work. Anne Kuper and Marti Weithman provided invaluable assistance preparing the report for publication. Human Rights Watch/Helsinki would like to thank the Governments of Azerbaijan and Armenia and the authorities of Nagorno-Karabakh for their cooperation. The authors would also like to thank all those who read and commented on the report.

---

[1]Formerly Helsinki Watch, Human Rights Watch/Helsinki has been monitoring the conflict connected with Nagorno-Karabakh since December 1990 and has issued two reports dealing directly with the fighting there: *Bloodshed in the Caucasus: Escalation of the Armed Conflict in Nagorno-Karabakh*, (New York:Human Rights Watch/Helsinki, September 1992), hereafter *Escalation of the Armed Conflict in Nagorno-Karabakh*; and "Bloodshed in the Caucasus: Indiscriminate Bombing and Shelling by Azerbaijani Forces in Nagorno-Karabakh," (New York: Human Rights Watch/Helsinki, Volume 5, Issue 10:July 1993), hereafter "Indiscriminate Bombing".

This report only covers military operations carried out in direct connection with fighting over Nagorno-Karabakh. Consequently, it does not deal with cross-border fighting and shelling between the Republics of Azerbaijan and Armenia. These topics, however, may serve as the subject of future reports.

In November 1991, the Azerbaijani Parliament annulled the autonomous status of Nagorno-Karabakh. The map in this text depicts the present provincial deliniations, with the border of Nagorno-Karabakh highlighted over that. Human Rights Watch/Helsinki takes no position on the ultimate status of Nagorno-Karabakh.

[2]The Azerbaijan government has renamed Stepanakert "Khankendi." For the sake of clarity, the report uses Stepanakert.

TABLE OF CONTENTS

SUMMARY

This Human Rights Watch/Helsinki report on the war over the Nagorno-Karabakh Autonomous Oblast[3] of Azerbaijan covers the period from the beginning of 1993 to September 1994[4] and examines violations of the rules of war by the three main parties to the conflict: the Azerbaijani army and forces under its control, the Nagorno-Karabakh army, and the Republic of Armenia army.

The war — the longest-running conflict in the former Soviet Union — is nearing the end of its seventh year. A shaky cease-fire achieved in May 1994 has left two large, well-equipped armies facing each other over a deserted landscape of empty villages and collective farms in the Azeri lowlands around Karabakh. An estimated 25,000 have been killed and over one million displaced and made refugees on both sides. In December 1994, the Conference on Security and Cooperation in Europe (CSCE) agreed to send a 3,000-strong multinational peacekeeping force to the conflict, but the details still must be worked out and the shaky ceasefire formalized into a truce.[5]

What began in early 1988 with demonstrations calling for the unification of the Republic of Armenia with Nagorno-Karabakh had become a full-scale war by 1992. In 1993, the war outgrew Karabakh itself, with almost all the fighting spilling over into Azerbaijan proper as Karabakh Armenian forces[6] conducted large-scale

---

[3]Although the Nagorno-Karabakh Autonomous Oblast of Azerbaijan declared independence in January 1992 as the Republic of Nagorno-Karabakh, no country recognizes this independence, and under international law the area remains part of Azerbaijan. In this report, "Nagorno-Karabakh" refers to the Nagorno-Karabakh Autonomous Oblast.

In the Soviet Union, an autonomous oblast was the second smallest administrative unit, subordinate either to an autonomous republic (e.g., North Ossetia) or to one of the fifteen union republic that constituted the U.S.S.R.

[4]There are some minor updates, including information on the Conference on Security and Cooperation in Europe's [CSCE] December 1994 decision to send to Karabakh a 3,000-strong multinational peacekeeping force.

[5] At its December 1994 summit, the CSCE renamed itself the OSCE, the Organization on Security and Cooperation in Europe.

[6]The war in Nagorno-Karabakh presents an interesting case for the use of ethnic identifiers. "Karabakh Armenians" is used to signify forces connected with the self-proclaimed, breakaway "Republic of Nagorno-Karabakh." "Karabakh Armenian" forces, however, may include citizens of the Republic of Armenia, mercenaries, and members of the armed forces of the Republic of Armenia. Only where it can be determined that soldiers in an action are overwhelmingly from the armed forces of the Republic of Armenia will the term "Armenian forces" or "Armenian soldiers" be used.

operations that resulted in the seizure of all the Azeri-populated provinces surrounding Karabakh on the south, west, and east and in the forcible displacement of the Azeri civilian population, some 450,000-500,000 individuals.[7] Karabakh Armenian forces occupy twenty to twenty-five percent of Azerbaijan.

Fighting in Karabakh took on new dimensions in 1994. Tractors and herds of sheep have given way to T-72 tanks, Grad missiles, heavy artillery, and SU-25 ground attack fighter planes. Casualties are counted in the tens of thousands. Fifty — even one hundred — men may be killed in just a few days to retake a single village or strategic height.

Because 1993 witnessed unrelenting Karabakh Armenian offensives against the Azerbaijani provinces surrounding Nagorno-Karabakh,[8] the vast majority of the violations during this period were the direct result of these offensive actions.[9] The Azeri civilian population was expelled from all areas captured by Karabakh Armenian forces, Azeri civilians caught by advancing Karabakh Armenian forces during their offensives of 1993 were taken hostage, and many Azeris were killed by indiscriminate fire as they attempted to escape. Wide-scale looting and destruction of civilian property accompanied these actions. Some instances of looting and pillaging, such as in Agdam, an Azeri city of some 50,000 that fell to Karabakh Armenian forces in July 1993, were organized and planned by the authorities of Nagorno-Karabakh.

Since late 1993, the conflict has also clearly become internationalized: in addition to Azerbaijani and Karabakh Armenian forces, troops from the Republic of Armenia participate on the Karabakh side in fighting inside Azerbaijan and in

---

[7] Throughout, "Azeri" will refer to those who are ethnically Azeri, such as an "Azeri women" or an "Azeri-populated village." "Azerbaijani" will refer to organizations connected with the Republic of Azerbaijan, such as the "Azerbaijani army." This division is arbitrary and limited to this paper.

According to Prof. Tadeusz Swietochowski, "Azerbaijani" was coined in the 1930s to refer to the inhabitants of the Soviet republic Azerbaijan. "Azeri" became the preferred term of use during the "perestroika" era and Popular Front period. There is no received, standardized usage.

[8] In 1993, Karabakh Armenian forces captured the following provinces of Azerbaijan: the remainder of Lachin province and all of Kelbajar, Agdam, Qubatli, Jebrayil, Fizuli, Zangelan, and part of Agjabedi and Terter provinces.

While Azeri forces launched a massive offensive in the latter part of December 1993, the majority of fighting took place in Azerbaijan proper and over areas already emptied of their civilian populations.

[9] Whichever side is on the offensive forces out the civilian population and loots and destroys homes and other civilian objects. Azerbaijani forces exhibited similar behavior during their June 1992 offensive against Mardakert province, Nagorno-Karabakh.

Karabakh.[10]

Karabakh Armenian violations of the rules of war for the period the report covers include the following: forced displacement of the Azeri population by means of indiscriminate and targeted shelling of civilian populations; capture of civilian stragglers; looting and burning of civilian homes; the taking and holding hostages; and the mistreatment and likely summary execution of prisoners of war and other captives.

The Republic of Armenia's violations of the rules of war for the period the report covers include grave breaches of the Geneva Conventions: holding hostages; and the likely killing of prisoners of war.[11] Armenian forces are also alleged to have taken hostages.

Azerbaijani violations of the rules of war during this period include indiscriminate use of air power resulting in civilian casualties; hostage-taking; and the mistreatment and likely execution of prisoners. Hostage-taking and mistreatment of prisoners of war are grave breaches of the Geneva Conventions.

Human Rights Watch/Helsinki takes no position concerning the ultimate political status of Nagorno-Karabakh. Our concerns center around violations of the rules of war, which all sides have committed during the many years of fighting.

---

[10]Afghan "mujahideen" and Slavic mercenaries also take part in the fighting. The Slavs on both sides, the Afghans for Azerbaijan.

In situations of armed conflict (international or not), Human Rights Watch is neutral on the use by either party of mercenary soldiers. We do, however, research and report on violations of the laws of war committed by mercenaries. For a fuller explanation of this policy, see Chapter VI.

[11]Grave breaches of the Geneva Conventions can be prosecuted as such only in international armed conflicts. Under international law, rebels cannot be charged with grave breaches. See Appendix A, International Law.

RECOMMENDATIONS

To the government of Azerbaijan:

1. Abide by the applicable humanitarian law rules for the victims of armed conflict, in particular,

(a) cease attacks on civilian populations and civilian objects, especially by aircraft without precision bombing devices that do not allow for accurate targeting;

(b) cease the inhumane treatment — including summary execution — of all persons placed "hors de combat;"

(c) immediately and unilaterally release all hostages, whether held in government custody or in private hands[12]; refrain from taking hostages, should future military operations take Azerbaijani forces into areas populated by Armenians.

2. Investigate and prosecute those persons suspected of grave breaches of the Geneva Conventions.

To the government of Armenia:

1. Abide by the applicable humanitarian law rules for the protection of victims of the armed conflict;

2. Investigate and prosecute those persons from the army of the Republic of Armenia or the Armenian Ministry of the Interior fighting in Karabakh and suspected of grave breaches of the Geneva Conventions, such as killing of prisoners and the taking and holding of hostages.

(a) allow an international investigation of the January 29, 1994 deaths of eight Azeri prisoners of war in custody of the army of the Republic of Armenia in Armenia; immediately release all autopsy reports and relevant findings; punish all culpable.

---

[12]Hostages in the conflict are held both by governments and by individuals. This applies to all parties.

To the authorities of Nagorno-Karabakh:

1. Abide by the applicable humanitarian law rules for the victims of armed conflict, in particular,

(a) cease attacks on the civilian population and civilian objects, especially by the use of such inaccurate weapons as Grad rocket launchers;

(b) cease forcibly displacing the Azeri civilian population from captured territories;

(c) cease the practice of hostage-taking; unilaterally and immediately release all hostages, including those in private hands;

(d) cease conducting a policy of "scorched earth" on captured enemy territory, particularly looting, pillaging, and burning of civilian objects; and

(e) cease the inhumane treatment — including summary execution — of all persons who are placed "hors de combat."

2. Prosecute those responsible for violations of the rules of war.

To the U.S. government:

1. Condemn forcefully and even-handedly violations of the rules of war by all parties in the conflict.

2. Call on the government of Armenia to investigate the deaths of eight Azeri prisoners of war on January 29, 1994;

3. Play a more active role in the OSCE Minsk Group peace talks;

4. Withhold aid — except humanitarian assistance — to all parties to the conflict.

To the government of Russia and the OSCE:

1. Ensure that any peace keeping or separation force will have neutral, multinational observers and a strong human rights mandate.

To the OSCE:

1. closely monitor compliance with the Conventional Forces in Europe Treaty to ensure that weapons in excess to those registered under the agreement do not enter the region and that registered weapons are not illegally transferred to combatants.

GEOGRAPHY-DEMOGRAPHICS-HISTORY

The ethnically Armenian Nagorno-Karabakh Autonomous Oblast comprises roughly 1,700 square miles of mountainous terrain in southwestern Azerbaijan. It is inside the international borders of Azerbaijan and shares no border with Armenia. In Russian, "Nagorno" means mountainous; in Turkish, "Karabakh" means black garden, referring to the fruitfulness of the land. Armenians call the region "Artsakh", while Azeris refer to it as "Yukhari Karabakh", literally "Upper Karabakh." The lowland areas surrounding Nagorno-Karabakh but not part of it are sometimes referred to as "Lower Karabakh." At the Lachin corridor, Karabakh's western border comes within six miles of the Republic of Armenia.

The area comprising Nagorno-Karabakh was incorporated by the Tsarist Empire in the early nineteenth century. The Persian Empire ceded it to Russia in 1813 under the Treaty of Gulistan, a town in present-day Azerbaijan on Karabakh's northern border where the agreement was signed. The Treaty of Turkmenchai in 1828 established what is now the present frontier between Azerbaijan and Iran.[13] Modern-day Karabakh was part of Elizavetopol Guberniya during Tsarist rule.

After the outbreak of the Russian revolution, the newly-founded republics of Armenia and Azerbaijan fought bitterly for control of Nagorno-Karabakh, with British troops briefly occupying Karabakh. In 1921, after the imposition of Soviet power in Transcaucasia,[14] the Bolsheviks awarded Nagorno-Karabakh to Azerbaijan in a decision hotly contested by Armenians.

Both Azeris and Armenians argue over the history of Nagorno-Karabakh. Located at the confluence of the Persian, Ottoman, and Russian empires, the area experienced countless invasions and population transfers as various migrations swept over the region. In one century one group could form a majority, in the next it could find itself a minority. According to the 1989 census, Nagorno-Karabakh's population was approximately 75 percent ethnic Armenian(145,000) and 25 percent ethnic Azeri (40,688).[15] Before the outbreak of hostilities, Stepanakert, the Oblast's capital, was

---

[13]Today, about fifteen million Azeris live across the border in Iran. The majority of Azerbaijan's population of 7 million is ethnically-Azeri, but there are substantial Talysh, Russian, and Lezgin communities.

[14]The term "Transcaucasia" is a Russian notion. The term refers to the land mass south of the Caucasus mountains, seen from a northern (Russian) perspective: modern-day Georgia, Azerbaijan, and Armenia. In Russian, "Zakavkaz'e" literally translates as "beyond the Caucasus."

[15]*Natsional'nyi Sostav Naseleniya SSSR, po dannym Vsesoyuznyi Perepisi Naseleniya 1989 g.*, Moskva, "Finansy i Stastika."

Armenians claim that the Azerbaijani government was intentionally tilting the

largely Armenian, while Shusha, Karabakh's pre-Soviet center, was comprised mostly of Azeris. Although granted the status of an autonomous oblast in Azerbaijan, Armenians living in Karabakh alleged that they suffered discrimination and had little decision-making power. The Azerbaijani government claims that median income was higher in Karabakh than in the rest of Azerbaijan. In 1988, demonstrations in both Yerevan, Armenia and Stepanakert, the capital of Nagorno-Karabakh, called for a union of the two territories. Violence quickly broke out, degenerating into a full-scale war by early 1992.

By mid-1992, Karabakh Armenian troops had forced out all of Nagorno-Karabakh's Azeri population. There are no current population figures for the Armenian population in Karabakh; estimates run from 100,000-160,000, with Karabakh Armenian authorities stressing the higher figure. Tens of thousands of ethnic Armenians fled Azerbaijani advances in Nagorno-Karabakh's Mardakert province in the second half of 1992; most, however, have returned to Nagorno-Karabakh.

Azeris are for the most part Shiite Muslims, though some are Sunni. Armenians practice Apostolic Christianity. The Azerbaijani language closely resembles Anatolian Turkish; Armenian is an Indo-European language having a unique alphabet. Karabakh Armenian and the Armenian spoken in the Republic of Armenia differ greatly, though are mutually understandable.

---

demographic balance through Azeri in-migration and point to a 1959 census in which Armenians comprised 85 percent of Karabakh's population. Azeris believe that the 1989 census under-represented Azeris because many had already left Karabakh.

I. IMMEDIATE BACKGROUND TO THE CONFLICT, FEBRUARY 1988-MARCH 1993[16]

The genesis of the current war in Nagorno-Karabakh dates back to February 1988, when Armenians in Stepanakert, the capital of Nagorno-Karabakh, held demonstrations demanding Nagorno-Karabakh's incorporation into Armenia. This demand was taken up by the Karabakh Oblast Soviet, which voted to appeal to the USSR Supreme Soviet for incorporation into the Republic of Armenia. Demonstrations by Armenians in Yerevan, the capital of Armenia, in support of their ethnic brethren and continued rallies in Stepanakert prompted intervention by Soviet troops and triggered waves of pogroms and violent deportations of Armenians from Azerbaijan and Azeris from Armenia.[17]

The most brutal of these events was the anti-Armenian pogrom in Sumgait, Azerbaijan, which took the lives of thirty-two Armenians, wounded hundreds more, and intensified the fears of ethnic Armenians living in other parts of Azerbaijan. In November 1988, anti-Armenian riots once again broke out, in the former Kirovabad, today's Ganje, in central Azerbaijan.

The Armenian Supreme Soviet voted on June 15, 1988, to accept Nagorno-Karabakh into the Republic of Armenia. The Azerbaijani Supreme Soviet responded the following day, voting not to relinquish the region. In July 1988, the USSR government debated and then rejected Armenian demands for incorporation. Two months later, renewed clashes between Armenians and Azeris in Stepanakert sent nearly all of the capital's Azeri population fleeing from the city. The USSR government placed Nagorno-Karabakh under Moscow's direct rule in January 1989, but this stopped neither clashes between residents and government authorities (mainly USSR Interior Ministry troops), nor clashes between Azeris and Armenians. Soviet troops and tanks were deployed in Stepanakert in May 1989 to put down a general strike, in which protesters again called for unification of Nagorno-Karabakh with Armenia and an end to new Azeri settlements in the region.

The Azerbaijani desire for continued rule over Nagorno-Karabakh helped galvanize the Azerbaijani Popular Front, which in August 1989 declared a boycott of

---

[16]The section covering the events of 1988-91 is taken with minor changes from Human Rights Watch/Helsinki's September 1992 report *Escalation of the Armed Conflict in Nagorno-Karabakh*.

[17]From 1988 through 1990 an estimated 300,000-350,000 Armenians either fled under threat of violence or were deported from Azerbaijan, and roughly 167,000 Azeris were forced to flee Armenia, often under violent circumstances.

Armenia and spearheaded a railway blockade of Armenia and Nagorno-Karabakh.[18] Three months later, Moscow ceased its direct rule over Nagorno-Karabakh, and returned control to local authorities. In January 1990 USSR troops stormed Baku, the Azerbaijani capital, purportedly to protect Armenians. Many observers believe the real goal was to crush the Popular Front. The crackdown did not prevent violent reprisals against Armenians: anti-Armenian pogroms in January resulted in the deaths of about sixty-eight Armenians; moreover, the Soviet troops used brutal force in Baku, killing about one hundred Azeri residents, most of them unarmed.[19]

Armenians in both Armenia and Nagorno-Karabakh continued to reject the Azerbaijani claim to Nagorno-Karabakh. One month after the August 1991 "putsch" in Moscow, which ended communist rule in the Soviet Union, the Nagorno-Karabakh Oblast Soviet and the governing council of the Geranboi (Shaumyan)[20] District (located north of Nagorno-Karabakh Oblast), announced the establishment of the Nagorno-Karabakh Republic and declared that it was no longer under Azerbaijani jurisdiction.

In November 1991 the Azerbaijani parliament, facing increasingly fierce popular demands for decisive action in Nagorno-Karabakh, voted to annul Nagorno-Karabakh's status of autonomous oblast. The Nagorno-Karabakh parliament responded by holding a referendum on independence in which an overwhelming majority of residents voted in favor of independence from Azerbaijan. On January 6, 1992, the Nagorno-Karabakh "Republic" parliament declared independence from Azerbaijan.

Beginning in 1988 the issue of Nagorno-Karabakh shaped the movements within both Armenia and Azerbaijan for greater independence of their respective republics from the USSR. The Karabakh Committee, which led the movement in Armenia for democratization and for an independent Karabakh, eventually was renamed the Armenian National Movement. Its leader, Levon Ter-Petrosyan, was elected the first non-communist chairman of the Armenian Supreme Soviet in July 1990. He is currently Armenia's president. The Popular Front of Azerbaijan gained popularity because of its tough stand on Nagorno-Karabakh. The conflict has ousted from power two of Azerbaijan's presidents because of their military shortcomings: Ayaz Mutalibov in 1992 and Abulfaz Elchibey in 1993.

The level of violence in Nagorno-Karabakh and surrounding districts

---

[18]Azerbaijani economic and transport blockades against both Armenia and Nagorno-Karabakh continued sporadically until the summer of 1991, when a full and permanent blockade was effected.

[19]*See Conflict in the Soviet Union: Black January in Azerbaijan.* (New York:Helsinki Watch/Memorial Report, May 1991).

[20]Geranboi is the official Azeri name for the province. Shaumyan the unofficial Armenian one.

increased steadily during the course of the above events, despite occasional lulls. In the wake of the February 1988 demonstrations, Armenian and Azeri residents engaged in communal violence, characterized by individual attacks, "mainly at night, aimed at destroying livestock and harassing people. There was also hostage-taking, which frightened people in neighboring villages."[21] Stoning passing cars also became common.

This kind of violence intensified toward the end of 1989, as Armenians staged strikes in Nagorno-Karabakh to protest the Azerbaijani blockade of that region, as well as of Armenia.[22] On January 15, 1990, roughly 17,000 additional troops of the USSR Ministry of Interior (MVD) were sent to the region to enforce a state of emergency declared the same day in Nagorno-Karabakh and at the Armenian-Azerbaijani border.[23] At least twice during the spring of 1990 these troops used force to put down demonstrations by Armenians who claimed they were unarmed. By the summer of 1990 Soviet military checkpoints had been set up on all roads leading to Stepanakert, and travel within Nagorno-Karabakh generally was reported to be under Soviet military control.

Raids on villages and shoot-outs between armed bands of Armenians and Azeris became a frequent occurrence, especially in the districts of Azerbaijan that border Nagorno-Karabakh to the north. An estimated 115 attacks on law enforcement officials, military outposts and military patrols took place between January and May 1991.[24]

An increasingly open flow of arms apparently facilitated the formation of paramilitary self-defense forces of ethnic Armenians, leading to sporadic armed clashes between Armenians and Azeris in the region. A watershed came in the spring and summer of 1991, when Azerbaijani Special Function Militia Troops, or OMON, accompanied by Soviet Army troops, conducted a passport[25] and arms check known

---

[21]Ramiz Melikov, deputy press secretary of the Azerbaijani Ministry of Defense, interviewed by Human Rights Watch/Helsinki in Baku.

[22]Indeed, Soviet officials characterizing the level of violence in the region said that not a day went by "without gunfire, explosives, mine blasts, arson, and pogroms." *See* David Remnick, "Soviet Official Warns of 'Homemade Lebanon.'" *The Washington Post*, October 2, 1989, p. A23.

[23]Although the state of emergency was declared in response to the violence in Baku, inexplicably it was not declared in Baku itself.

[24]Moscow TASS International Service in Russian, FBIS, May 6, 1991.

[25]Every citizen of the former Soviet Union had an internal passport which included, among other things, his or her residence permit, or *propiska*. In order to move to another town or village, a citizen had to obtain a propiska for the new location; without a propiska one could be deported from an area.

as "Operation Ring" in Armenian villages in Nagorno-Karabakh and the Khanlar and Geranboi (Shaumyan) districts of Azerbaijan. "Operation Ring" resulted in the arrest and detention of hundreds of Armenian men, the temporary deportation of thousands of Armenians, and the emptying of between twenty-two and twenty-four Armenian villages. It was reportedly carried out with an unprecedented degree of violence and a systematic violation of human rights.

Azerbaijani Internal Ministry officials claimed that the passport check was necessary because Armenians were illegally moving to Nagorno-Karabakh[26] and the Khanlar and Geranboi (Shaumyan) districts in order to increase artificially the Armenian population of these locations and to participate in armed insurrection. Azerbaijani and Soviet forces sought to seize illegal weapons and apprehend members of Armenian paramilitary groups; the participation of the Soviet Army was deemed necessary to "prevent massive armed action, to get rid of bandits."[27] According to the USSR press, the operation led to the confiscation of a variety of weapons from both Armenians and Azeris.

Armenians maintain that the aim of these attacks was to deport Armenians from the villages of Nagorno-Karabakh and from the Khanlar and Geranboi (Shaumyan) districts, and that the entire operation was a preparation for war carried out under USSR President Mikhail Gorbachev's orders. In response to Operation Ring and as a result of the rapid collapse of the Soviet Union, skirmishes between Armenian and Azerbaijani forces became more frequent in Nagorno-Karabakh and bordering districts. In the late summer and early autumn 1991 Armenians fought to retake their villages, and Azeris used force to counter Nagorno-Karabakh's declaration of independence. The number of casualties and hostages began to mount rapidly.

After the formal break-up of the Soviet Union in December 1991, USSR MVD troops, believed by some to have had some mitigating effect on the hostilities, withdrew from Nagorno-Karabakh, leaving Armenian and Azerbaijani forces in more direct conflict with each other. The dissolution of the USSR also adversely affected control over, and discipline within, Soviet armed forces. Heavy artillery, rocket-propelled grenades (RPGs), rocket launchers, tanks, and armed personnel carriers, property of the Soviet Army, were either sold to, loaned to, or otherwise found their way into the hands of combatants on both sides, making the armed conflict even more lethal.

Karabakh erupted into full-scale war in 1992 as weapons poured into the region and Soviet Interior Ministry troops withdrew. The use of mercenaries on both sides was common, and many alleged that rogue Russian army units took part in combat. Four major events characterized the war in 1992: the massacre of hundreds of Azeri civilians in Khojali, NKAO, by Karabakh forces with alleged support of the

---

[26] That is, without a *propiska*, or residency permit.

[27] Helsinki Watch interview with Telman Khaliogly, then First Deputy Chairman of the Supreme Soviet of Azerbaijan, June 17, 1991.

366th Regiment of the Russian army; the Karabakh Armenian seizure of Shusha, the last Azeri-populated town in Karabakh (it served as a fire base for attacks on Stepanakert); the Karabakh Armenian capture of the Azerbaijani town of Lachin and the six-mile "corridor" between Nagorno-Karabakh and Armenia; and the June 1992 Azerbaijani offensive against Mardakert province in Nagorno-Karabakh. Serious human rights violations by both sides characterized all the above actions.

Both sides shelled each other's cities and towns and committed atrocities. In February 1992, Karabakh Armenian forces — reportedly backed by soldiers from the 366th Motor Rifle Regiment of the Russian Army — seized the Azeri-populated town of Khojali, about seven kilometers outside of Stepanakert. More than 200 civilians were killed in the attack, the largest massacre to date in the conflict.[28]

In April, an Azerbaijani attack on Maraga reportedly took forty civilian lives and several dozen hostages. A month later, the Karabakh Armenians — again with alleged Russian support — seized Shusha, Karabakh's last Azeri-populated town. Later that month, Karabakh Armenian forces broke through to Armenia at the Azerbaijani town of Lachin, creating the so-called Lachin corridor. At Lachin, roughly ten kilometers separates Armenia from Karabakh.

In June 1992, however, a large-scale Azerbaijani offensive against the Geranboi (Shaumyan) region of Azerbaijan and Mardakert province in Nagorno-Karabakh achieved initial success. Armed with heavy weapons received after the division of the Soviet army's arsenal under the Treaty of Tashkent of May 1992, the Azeri army captured nearly 80 percent of Mardakert province and created nearly 40,000 ethnic Armenian refugees.[29] The Azeri forces subjected the Armenians in Karabakh — including civilians — to a withering air and artillery bombardment during the summer of 1992. By September, however, the Karabakh Armenian position had stabilized.

In February 1993, a large-scale Karabakh Armenian offensive in the Mardakert region recaptured numerous villages as well as the Sarsang reservoir, severing the Terter-Kelbajar road and cutting-off Kelbajar province from the rest of Azerbaijan except for the Omar Pass over the Murov mountains.[30] This attack

---

[28]There are no exact figures for the number of Azeri civilians killed because Karabakh Armenian forces gained control of the area after the massacre. While it is widely accepted that 200 hundred Azeris were murdered, as many as 500-1,000 may have died.

[29]Mardakert was largely Armenian.

[30]Aidyn Mekhtiyev, "Vspyshka Aktivnosti na Armyano-Azerbaidzhanskom Fronte," *Nezavisimaya Gazeta,* Moscow, February 2, 1993, p. 3. On February 5, Baku Radio reported that most of the region south of the Sarsang reservoir had fallen to Armenian forces, including the villages of Srkhavend, Chldran, Pogosagomer, and Kochohot; by the end of the month, Armenian forces were north of the reservoir and thus in control of the Sarsang hydroelectric plant.

reversed most advances the Azerbaijani Army made during its offensive in the Mardakert region of Nagorno-Karabakh in 1992. Fighting in that region took place in a landscape of depopulated ethnic Armenian villages, and consequently did not directly affect civilian populations.[31] Skirmishing and artillery duels also took place on other fronts, including around Agdam and Fizuli.

The Karabakh Armenian offensive in Mardakert in February 1993 achieved three important goals: Azeri forces were pushed out of a large portion of Mardakert, allowing for the return of the ethnic Armenian population;[32] an important source of power, the Sarsang reservoir and hydroelectric station, was secured;[33] Karabakh Armenian forces seized Kelbajar's eastern flank, cutting off its main outlet to Azerbaijan, the Terter-Kelbajar road.

The speed and scale of Azeri defeats set off a political crisis in Azerbaijan, a prelude to the events leading to the ouster of elected Popular Front President Elchibey several months later. On February 9 and 10, 1993, the Popular Front government accused the commander of the Mardakert region and a war hero to Azeris, Col. Surat Huseinov, of inadequately defending the region and of ordering the withdrawal of heavy weapons and units from the area.[34] On February 23, 1993, Huseinov was relieved of his command as well as his title of "Plenipotentiary Presidential Representative" in the Mardakert region.[35] In June 1993, Col. Huseinov led a military force that ousted President Elchibey from power.

By March, the Azerbaijani army — never a well-organized or well-commanded force — was in disarray. Calls were made for soldiers to return to their

---

[31]The population of the Mardakert region, largely Armenian, fled *en masse* from a large-scale Azeri offensive that began in June 1992.

[32]According to the Azerbaijani Defense Ministry, some Azeri refugees relocated to the Mardakert region in 1992 had to be evacuated in 1993. See Human Rights Watch/Helsinki's "Indiscriminate Bombing."

[33]February 6, 1993, Baku Radio, Baku, in FBIS-SOV-93-024, 2-8-93, p. 51; February 25, 1993, Moscow Interfax, in FBIS-SOV-93-036, February 25, 1993, p. 74; February 25, 1993, Yerevan Radio, Yerevan, in FBIS-SOV-93-037, p. 50.
The capture of the hydroelectric station at Sarsang provided the Karabakh Armenians a reliable source of power. As of Spring 1994, electric power operates much more reliably in Karabakh than in Armenia proper, a source of immeasurable pride to the local population.

[34]Aidyn Mekhtiyev, "Narodnyi Front Obvinyayet Voennykh," *Nezavisimaya Gazeta*, Moscow, February 12, 1993, p. 1.

[35]2-23-93, Moscow Radio Rossii, in FBIS-SOV-93-034, February 23, 1993, p.58.
On February 20, Azerbaijan's defense minister, Rakhim Gaziyev, resigned under pressure, replaced by Gen. Dadash Rizayev.

units or face "serious punishments."[36] The head of Azerbaijan's Defense Ministry's Information and Analytical Center blamed February 1993's setbacks on the fact that "the National Army of Azerbaijan was lately drawn into political games."[37]

In early March 1993, in an interview with the *Boston Globe*, Nagorno-Karabakh's Defense Minister Serge Sarkissian commented that his troops were "on the move" against a demoralized Azerbaijani army riven by factionalism.[38] According to him, it would be a matter of time before his forces liberated all of Karabakh. In June 1993, Sarkissian became Defense Minister of Armenia, a post he still holds.

---

[36] 2-21-93, Baku Radio, Baku, in FBIS-SOV-93-033, 2-23-93, p. 45.

[37] 2-22-93, Moscow Itar-Tass, in FBIS-SOV-93-033, February 22, 1993, p. 47.

[38] John Auerbach, "Passions run deep as Armenians, Azeris fight on in Forgotten War," *Boston Globe*, March 9, 1993, p. 1.

II. VIOLATIONS OF THE RULES OF WAR, APRIL 1993 - FEBRUARY 1994

During 1993, the vast majority of violations of the rules of war, such as indiscriminate fire, the destruction of civilian objects, the taking of hostages, and looting, were the direct result of Karabakh Armenian offensives — often supported by forces from the Republic of Armenia. These offensives resulted in the capture of all Azeri-populated provinces surrounding Nagorno-Karabakh on the east, west, and south and the expulsion of the civilian Azeri population. The following section sets out these violations in the context of the main Karabakh Armenian offensives of 1993. Other violations that both sides committed such as the mistreatment of prisoners are covered in thematic sections.

THE SEIZURE OF KELBAJAR BY KARABAKH ARMENIAN FORCES - APRIL 1993

Rather than capture the rest of Karabakh as Sarkissian predicted, Karabakh Armenian forces — with alleged Russian and Armenian military support — seized all of the Kelbajar Province of Azerbaijan in a "blitzkrieg" operation that began March 27 and ended by April 5.[39] During this offensive, they committed several violations of the rules of war, including forced displacement of the civilian population, indiscriminate fire, and the taking of hostages.

At the time of the offensive, mountainous Kelbajar province was largely cut off from the rest of Azerbaijan. Armenia lay to the west, the Lachin corridor (captured by Karabakh Armenian forces in June 1992) to the south, Mardakert province (with its vital Terter-Kelbajar road in Karabakh Armenian hands) to the east, and to the north, the Murov mountains reaching heights of over 10,000 feet towered over the province. Because of prior Karabakh Armenian land conquests, the only outlet from Kelbajar to Azerbaijan proper was over the Murov mountains to the north through the Omar pass, a treacherous journey in winter.

---

[39] Eyewitnesses reported artillery fire with a trajectory originating in Armenia falling on Kelbajar city.

In addition, the Azerbaijani government stated that radio intercepts proved that mountain troops from the 128th Regiment of the 7th Russian Army based in Armenia took part in the battle.

See Aydyn Mekhtiyev, "Armyanskiye Voiska zanyali Kel'badzhar," *Nezavisimaya Gazeta*, Moscow, April 6, 1994, p. 3.

Reportedly, Mahmoud Al-Said, UN Representative in Baku, Azerbaijan, and a fluent Russian speaker, listened to the tapes and confirmed that native Russian speakers were on it.

An estimated 60,000 individuals — equally divided among Kurds and Azeris — lived in Kelbajar province before the offensive.[40] In the space of a week, 60,000 people were forced to flee their homes. Today all are displaced, and Kelbajar stands empty and looted.

The swift and short nature of the Kelbajar offensive, the mountainous terrain with few good roads over which it was fought, and the late winter timing of the attack left the civilian population extremely vulnerable; many were taken hostage or killed by indiscriminate fire. Even though most expected a Karabakh Armenian move against Kelbajar, civilians had little or no advance warning of the actual attack and even less time to make their escape after the limited routes still available were closed by advancing Karabakh Armenian forces. The Azerbaijani army put up little resistance, often melting away into the civilian population. Many Karabakh Armenian units fired on escaping civilians, sometimes mistaking them for retreating Azerbaijani forces.

The attack on Kelbajar province began on March 26 or 27 from the east and south.[41] Azeri civilians were attacked, a violation of the prohibition on targeting civilians.[42] On March 27 Isa, a sixty-year-old collective farm administrator from Takhtabashi in the far east of Kelbajar province, close to the border with Karabakh, and several of his fellow villagers, all civilians and unarmed, were attacked on the way to a funeral:

> On the morning of March 27, I was riding on horseback with my brother Ahad and our friend Hussein, to the funeral of a relative in Chirakli. Suddenly a burst of machinegun fire opened up on us from the direction of Vankli, a neighboring [Karabakh[43]]

---

[40]Despite Armenian reports to the contrary, there is no evidence to support allegations that Kurds living either in Lachin or Kelbajar provinces supported the Armenian seizure of those areas or that large numbers of Kurds remained in the provinces after they fell to Armenian forces and sought to set up an autonomous Kurdish region. All Kurds fled, together with the Azeri population.

See "You too, Armenia," *Kurdish Life*, Brooklyn, New York. No. 9, Winter 1994.

[41]According to Afak, a thirty-four-year-old librarian of Kelbajar, Azeri villagers near Agdaban and Veng, close to the front with Karabakh, appeared in Kelbajar on March 27 and 28 seeking refuge from the fighting. Interview, refugee camp, Barda, Azerbaijan, March 31, 1993.

First names or pseudonyms are mostly used in the report for those who gave us testimony. The names of the dead as well as hostages and prisoners still held but not interviewed by Human Rights Watch/Helsinki are real. The names of Armenian prisoners of war interviewed in Azerbaijani detention are also real.

All information on prisoners and hostages is current as of April 1994 unless otherwise stated.

[42]*See* Appendix A, International Law.

Armenian-held village close to our village. My brother and
Hussein managed to escape, but my horse was killed and I had to
hide by some rocks. A short time later I could see another group
from our village on the way to the funeral. The [Karabakh]
Armenians opened up on them too, killing four and wounding one.
Yusuf Zeinalov, Habil Nabiyev, Mehman Musayev, and Yusuf
Azizov were all killed.[44]

Around noon, Isa's brother arrived with members of the village self-defense
force to retrieve the bodies of those killed. Shooting lasted until 5:00 P.M., when
according to Isa, three Karabakh Armenian BMPs[45] appeared from the direction of
Vanklu. "By that time we knew all was lost, and everyone ran back to village. We all
thought of one thing: how to save the children. By 6:00 P.M. on March 27 we were out
of Takhtibashi. The BMPs started to fire at us, but we escaped and headed towards the
tunnel near Zulfugarli."

Looting and destruction of civilian property are also prohibited[46] but occurred
frequently during the offensive. For instance, Isa sent his family through the tunnel and
decided to return to Takhtabasi at around 8:30 P.M. on the night of March 29, hoping
to save some cows he owned. When he returned to the village he saw several houses
had been looted by the Karabakh Armenians. The houses of his brother, Nowruz, and
of his cousin were burning. Another village, Galanboyu, in Kelbajar province, was
first shelled on March 30 from the direction of Narishli and Beylik and later looted and
burned by Karabakh Armenian forces, according to residents Erzani, sixty, and Yasin,
twenty-five, a teacher.

People started to leave, trying to escape through the tunnel near
Zulfugarli. But they quickly returned and said that the tunnel was
closed. We went to Zulfugarli village at around 2:00 P.M. on
March 30, remaining there until 9:00 pm. We headed back towards
Galanboyu and could see houses in the village burning. Maybe ten
or eleven of the fifty houses in our village were on fire. Safter

---

[43] The interviewees used the term *armiane*, "Armenians," or *armianskiye soldaty*,
"Armenian soldiers" in Russian or *Ermeniler* in Azeri. When later asked if they knew the
identity of the soldiers, they stated the identities. In cases where no identity could be
determined, Karabakh Armenian is used according to usage guidelines in footnote 6.

[44]Interview, refugee camp, Barda, Azerbaijan, March 31, 1994.

[45]Soviet-made armored personnel carriers. Depending on the model, they can be armed with
light and heavy machineguns, small caliber cannons (73mm), and anti-tank missiles.

[46]*See* Appendix A, International Law.

> Alishev's house was on fire, so was Shakkmali Ismailov's. When
> we tried to actually enter the village, we heard rifle and
> machinegun fire. We ran about a kilometer or two away to
> Gatergali hill that overlooks Galanboyu and stayed there until about
> 2:00 P.M. on March 31st. March 31st was sunny, so you could see
> soldiers looting the houses. Some were herding livestock out of the
> village; others were taking carpets and other belongings out of the
> houses and grouping them on the ground outside.[47]

While Karabakh Armenian forces initially allowed the majority of Kelbajar
province's civilian population to flee, after a time it seems most escape routes, except
those over the treacherous Murov mountains, were closed. It was at this time,
approximately between March 31 and April 1, that numerous Azerbaijani civilians
were either taken hostage or wounded or killed.

Civilians fleeing over the Murov mountains were targeted by Karabakh
Armenian forces. On March 31, the men from Galanboyu village referred to above
decided to flee over the mountain through which the Zulfugarli tunnel runs and then
head north towards the Murov mountains. Karabakh Armenians shot at them.

> We reached Gostas mountain and started to climb over it. Other
> people must have had the same idea, there were about one hundred
> of us. Azerbaijani soldiers were there too, trying to escape like
> everyone else. People were running through the snow, falling,
> calling out to one another. The wind was horrible. From time to
> time the [Karabakh] Armenians would see us — they seemed to
> have a position near Lachin village — and fire at us and shell with
> Grads[48] and machine guns. On April 1 we had reached Saridash

---

[47] Interview, Barda, Azerbaijan, April 2, 1994.

[48] The BM-21 rocket launcher, commonly referred to as the "Grad", has been widely deployed
during the course of the conflict. It is not very accurate, and its deployment in Karabakh has
resulted in numerous civilian casualties. Protocol I Additional to the Geneva Conventions clearly
states, however, that the means used in an attack must be carefully chosen to minimize civilian
casualties. See Appendix A, International Law.

In 1992, Azeri forces rained "Grads" on Stepanakert from Shusha, and in 1993
Armenian forces deployed "Grads" against villages to force the civilian population to flee. Most
Azeri civilians who suffered from indiscriminate fire in 1993 and 1994 named the highly
inaccurate "Grad" as the weapon used.

A descendant of the famous "Stalin Organ," the "Grad" is a fairly primitive rocket
fired singularly or in salvos from the back of a truck to stop large-scale infantry attacks. It has
a distinctive whine and whistle in its trajectory before it explodes, and therefore can be extremely
effective in provoking panic among civilians and poorly-trained troops.

village. We could see the Qamishli bridge that crosses the Terter
river. [Karabakh] Armenian forces had closed the bridge. We
continued on, and the growing fog helped our escape. By the night
of April 2 we reached Yanshaq village. Everyone was cold,
miserable, and tired. Many had frostbite.[49]

In a separate incident, on the morning of April 1, Karabakh Armenian forces
armed with automatic rifles and rocket-propelled grenades indiscriminately attacked
a Gaz-52 truck carrying approximately twenty-five Azerbaijani civilians (and no
soldiers) as it neared the tunnel between the villages of Zulfugarli and Jomerd.
According to a seventeen-year-old Azeri from Kelsali village, all the passengers but
one were shot or hit by shrapnel and then taken hostage:

> We didn't know that the [Karabakh] Armenians had closed the
> tunnel. It was light; we couldn't see any [Karabakh] Armenians, but
> we saw a BMP knocked out of action by the entrance to the tunnel.
> We were all civilians, our relatives were on the truck. We heard
> some shots, maybe they were trying to warn us. We didn't think that
> [Karabakh] Armenians had reached this far. All of a sudden there
> was shooting and explosions. The truck stopped. The driver in the
> cabin, Aslan Mirzayev, and his daughter, Afat, were killed
> instantly. My sister died also. When we were taken away she was
> lying wounded in the truck; later some [Karabakh] Armenian
> soldiers told us she had died. One of my brothers, Islam, was badly
> wounded — he died later, I buried him myself. When the
> [Karabakh] Armenian soldiers approached the truck they said they
> did not know we were civilians. They gave us medical help, then
> took us to Drombon, in the Mardakert region.[50]

Another brother of this witness was badly wounded on the truck, but
survived. He and two other family members, sisters, were taken hostage at that time

---

[49]Interview, Barda, Azerbaijan, April 2, 1994. Although some Azeri soldiers were present
when the Armenians took aim, the civilians greatly outnumbered the soldiers and therefore,
under the principle of proportionality, the Armenians were under a duty to hold their fire. *See*
Appendix A, International Law.

[50]Interview, April 14, 1994.

and exchanged later in 1993. They returned to Baku.[51]

By March 29 or 30 Karabakh Armenian forces — with reported assistance from Republic of Armenian forces — had encircled the city of Kelbajar and seized the heights around it. According to Ali, an electrician who worked on communications for the governor of Kelbajar province, Karabakh Armenian units called the governor on March 28 and gave him two days to surrender the city.[52]

Afak, one witness who was in the city until March 30, said Kelbajar was shelled the last few days before it fell, damaging civilian areas.

> On March 27 some missiles flew over the city but didn't seem to hit the town. The next day, the shells really started to fall in the city, closer to the Armenian border at the west end of town. We would go down to the basement; when the shells would roar overhead the house would start to shake and windows would break. There was a helicopter pad about 400 meters from my house; also a military unit about the same distance. But the area around my house were all civilian dwellings. There was no major damage right around my house, but a little farther on my neighbor Jengiz's house was burning. Jengiz's daughter Gunlari was wounded by a Grad missile. Ali Yusubov's house had also been destroyed.[53]

Artillery fire — either Karabakh Armenian or Armenian — damaged the Kelbajar hospital, according to Nejef, who remained in his native city until around 8:30 P.M. on March 31.

> Some of the shelling seemed to be coming from Armenia, from the direction of Vardenis.[54] These shells were hitting some cliffs by the helicopter pad. While we were there on March 30 about seven or eight shells hit this area. My family couldn't be evacuated that day

---

[51]Human Rights Watch/Helsinki spoke with the released brothers and sister in Baku, Azerbaijan on April 4, 1994. The brother had a severe bullet wound on his left thigh, with a scar approximately seven inches in length. According to the brother, their sister who was released is still in the hospital because of wounds received.

Another two sisters were in the truck and were also wounded; one had scars from wounds to the right arm and leg; the other, wounds to the left hand and fingers of the left hand as well as the right hip. Both were still hostages as of April 1994.

[52]Interview, Barda, Azerbaijan, March 31, 1994.

[53]Interview, Barda, Azerbaijan, March 31, 1994.

[54]Vardenis is an Armenian city about twenty-five kilometers west of Kelbajar.

and had to come back the next. On our way home we passed the
hospital. One of its wings was destroyed by shelling; the staff were
carrying out wounded.[55]

A journalist in the city at the time observed that the bombardment —
especially from Grad Rockets — was fired into Kelbajar city from the west, from
inside Armenia.[56]

Faced with the reality that Kelbajar would fall, the Azeri government
mounted a chaotic helicopter evacuation of those left in the city to spare them the
brutal trek over the Murov mountains. Though the airlift was supposedly limited to
civilians, soldiers sometimes forced their way on flights. A Caucasus-based
American journalist in Kelbajar during the offensive and evacuated by helicopter
wrote that,

> By Thursday afternoon, April 1, a fleet of six ME-8 civilian
> helicopters, designed to carry a maximum load of thirty, managed
> to extract several thousand women and children by doubling and
> trebling their loads. The helicopters were forced to swoop through
> a narrow canyon to reach a tiny, shell-pocked landing pad and then
> fly over a 4,000 meter mountain range to return to their base in the
> Azerbaijani city of Yevlakh, about an hour away. . . even if most of
> the civilian population is now gone or on its way out the situation
> in Kelbajar is certainly desperate.[57]

On noon on April 1, the last helicopter flight left Kelbajar, and no more
evacuation attempts were made because of the increased shelling around the helicopter
pad.[58] By April 3, Karabakh Armenian forces were in complete control of Kelbajar.
According to an Armenian journalist at the scene, Avet Demuryan, the majority of
civilians left in Kelbajar were allowed to flee north. Eighty civilians, however, were
taken hostage and sent to Stepanakert to be exchanged for Armenians in Azeri
captivity; some 150 soldiers were captured.[59]

Another wave of scared, cold, and exhausted displaced persons made its way

---

[55]Interview, Yevlakh, Azerbaijan, April 2, 1994.

[56]Thomas Goltz, "Azeri Air Lift," April 1993, unpublished. Also interview with author,
March 1994.

[57]Ibid.

[58]Moscow Itar-Tass, April 1, 1993, in FBIS-SOV-93-061, April 1, 1993, p. 72.

[59]"Armenians capture Key Azerbaijani City," The Washington Post, April 5, 1993, p. a13.

north over the Murov mountains after the fall of the city of Kelbajar. In all, thousands trekked over the Murov mountains to escape the Karabakh Armenian offensive. One report estimated that 200 Azeris died, mostly from exposure, during the mountain crossing.[60] Some fleeing Azeris tried to hide in the mountains or simply got lost and were taken hostage. One man from Bozliyu village reported that he and seven others took some sheep and hid on Karademak mountain for over a month. "The meat from the animals kept us alive. Plus I would sneak back to my house. Finally, on May 5, 1993, after almost a month, a Karabakh Armenian patrol took us hostage."[61]

The Azerbaijani government, with aid from the UNHCR and ICRC, set up centers to process those made homeless by the Karabakh Armenian offensive. Less than a week after the fall of the Kelbajar province, on April 7, 1993 the Azeri State Committee on Refugees reported registering 9,582 families from Kelbajar.[62] The displaced from the Kelbajar offensive were housed in schools, summer camps, and hotels, and also in tents.

The last Azeri displaced person had not crossed the Murov mountains to safety when on April 4, Karabakh Armenian forces mounted a secondary offensive against Fizuli, fifteen kilometers southeast of Karabakh, and against Qubatli and Zangelan provinces, which lie to the southwest of Karabakh. Reports stated that Karabakh Armenian forces captured more than fifteen villages and drove to within two kilometers of Fizuli before the advance stopped.[63]

This offensive loosened another flow of Azeri displaced persons: by late April, for example, Western diplomats in Fizuli reported that the city was largely deserted. On May 1, 1993, Azeri officials reported that there were now 546,000 registered refugees and displaced persons in the republic.[64]

Over the next two months, the Azerbaijani government attempted to institute

---

[60]Oleg Schedrov. "Fighting Rages in Azerbaijan, Refugees in Danger." Reuters, April 5, 1993.

[61]Interview, Shusha Prison, Nagorno-Karabakh, April 15, 1994.
According to the interviewee, six of those taken hostage at that time have been released.

[62]Sokhbet Mamedov, " Azerbaidzhan: 10 tysyach semei stali bezhentsami," *Izvestiya*, Moscow, April 5, 1993, p. 1.

[63]"Armenians Capture Strategic Sites in Battle over Caucasus Enclaves," *The New York Times*, April 12, 1993, p. 12; Valerii Yakov, "Na Yugo-Zapadnom Fronte Bez Peremen," *Izvestiya*, Moscow, April 13, 1993, p.1.

[64]*Izvestiya*, May 7, 1993, p. 1.
This official figure of 546,000 broke down as follows: 200,000 refugees from Armenia; 295,000 displaced persons from Karabakh and the regions bordering Karabakh; plus Meskhetian Turks that had sought shelter in Azerbaijan from unrest in Uzbekistan.

some military reforms, most of which had little real effect.[65]

U.N. SECURITY COUNCIL RESOLUTION 822 AND U.S.-RUSSIAN-TURKISH ATTEMPTS AT PEACE

By mid-April, international attention to the fighting in and around Karabakh brought a short lull to the battlefield that lasted until the end of June. On April 8, Finnish Col. Heiki Heppponen led a OSCE cease-fire monitoring mission to Baku.[66] The idea for such a mission had been worked out during the February 25-March 2,

---

[65]The fall of Kelbajar prompted the Azeri government to pass a string of restrictive measures in an ultimately futile effort to turn the course of the war. The fate of the former old guard communist President Ayaz Mutalibov was still fresh in the minds of President Elchibey and the members of his Popular Front Government: outrage over the February 1992 Armenian capture and subsequent massacre of at least two hundred civilians at Khojali, an Azeri village in Nagorno-Karabakh, had led to Mutalibov's ouster.

On April 2, 1993, President Elchibey issued a sixty-day state-of-emergency decree subsequently ratified by parliament. Among other things, the decree banned rallies and strikes, introduced censorship, and placed Baku under martial law. Military units patrolled the streets of Azerbaijan's capital.

Quick-fix steps were also taken to strengthen the military, which came under harsh criticism for the Kelbajar defeat. On April 4, the Azerbaijani Presidential Press Office issued the following statement:

> The main reason for Kelbajar's surrender to the enemy was the failure of the troops to comply with the command headquarter's order to defend the city. . . . The incident in Kelbajar has indicated that the level of morale and military preparedness is very low. . . . Another reason for our defeat in Kelbajar was the failure to get the military units organized in the form of an army.

Men born between 1958 and 1976 were forbidden to leave Azerbaijan, and induction points sprang up throughout the country. Press gangs inducted young men on the street, forcing them into waiting buses. A Russian journalist in Baku at the time described the following scene: "I fell into one of the conscription round-ups myself. The twenty-three-year-old young Azeri man escorting me almost ended up at the front. . . (along) with five scared young men sitting on a bus."

[66]Aidyn Mekhtiyev,"Voina v Azerbaidzhane idet svoim cheredom," *Nezvisimaya Gazeta*, Moscow, April 9, 1993, p.1.

The mission spent about two weeks in the area, visiting Azerbaijan, Armenia, and Nagorno-Karabakh.

For the complete mandate of the OSCE Advance Monitoring Group, see *COVCAS Bulletin*, Geneva, April 1, 1993, pp. 5-8.

1993 Minsk Group talks.[67] Two days later, President Yeltsin offered to mediate, and tripartite talks were held in Moscow.[68] On April 16, the authorities of Karabakh announced a unilateral cease-fire.[69] On April 21, while in Ankara, the presidents of Azerbaijan and Armenia agreed to continue work on the OSCE Minsk Group peace process.[70]

On April 30, the United Nations Security Council adopted Resolution 822, which called for a cease-fire, the withdrawal of "all occupying forces" from the Kelbajar region, the resumption of negotiations and open access for humanitarian efforts.[71] This resolution proved the impetus for an ambitious Russian-Turkish-United States peace initiative[72] that called for a withdrawal of forces from Kelbajar, a sixty-day cease-fire, the end of the energy blockade of Armenia, and continued peace talks.[73] Both Azerbaijan and Armenia accepted the plan, but the Karabakh Armenians refused.[74] Chairman of the Nagorno-Karabakh State Defense Committee Robert

---

[67]Carol Migdalovitz, "CRS Issue Brief: Armenia-Azerbaijan Conflict," Congressional Research Service, Washington, D.C., January 5, 1994, p.5.

The Minsk Group is the OSCE negotiation body tasked with bringing the war in Karabakh to an end. The group was formed in the Summer of 1992 under the leadership of the Italian diplomat Mario Raffaelli and was supposed to convene a peace conference in Minsk, Belorussia — hence the name. The group consists of eleven OSCE members, including the United States, France, Russia, Armenia, Azerbaijan, and Sweden. The present chairman is a Swede, Anders Bjurner, who replaced another Swedish diplomat, Jan Eliasson. See Chapter X, Peace Negotiations.

[68]Izvestiya, Moscow, April 10, 1994, p. 2.

[69]Arutyun Khachatryan, "Armeniya-Azerbaidzhan: Voina Nervov na Fone Tragedii," Russkaya Mysl', Paris, April 23-29, 1993.

[70]Migdalovitz, p. 5.

[71]United Nations Security Council, "Resolution 822 (1993)," s/RES/822 (1993), April 30, 1993.

[72]Elizabeth Fuller, "Russia's Diplomatic Offensive in the Transcaucasus," RFE/RL Research Report, October 1, 1993, p.5.

[73]"Armenia and Azerbaijan Agree on Peace Plan," The New York Times, May 27, 1993, p. a14.

[74]Reportedly large-scale demonstrations were held in Yerevan calling on President Ter-Petrosyan to reject the plan. See Sergei Bablyumyan, "Armeniya Podderzhala mezhdunarodnuyu initsiativu po
Karabakhu, Karabakh -net," Izvestiya, Moscow, May 27, 1993, p.1.

Kocharian commented, ". . . A peace-bringing to the region should take into account the essential interests of the Karabakh people."[75] On May 24 Azerbaijan declared a unilateral cease-fire.

The plan was modified, linking the withdrawal of Karabakh Armenian forces from occupied Azeri territory with additional guarantees for Karabakh's civilian population. Five hundred OSCE military observers were to monitor the plan.[76] Under pressure from Armenia's president Ter-Petrosyan, the Karabakh Armenians accepted the plan on June 14, 1993, but asked that implementation be deferred one month.[77] Karabakh Armenian forces seized Agdam, however, and consequently the resolution was never implemented.

KARABAKH ARMENIANS TAKE AGDAM-JULY 1993

The tripartite peace plan — along with Azerbaijani President Abulfez Elchibey — fell victim to the political chaos and military disorganization that engulfed Azerbaijan in June 1993. A coup led by the popular army commander Surat Huseinov toppled President Elchibey and his Popular Front government, bringing back to power Heidar Aliyev, the former Azerbaijani Communist Party boss.[78]

---

[75]He continued, "Because of that, Karabakh leadership's answer to the trilateral initiative is a call upon the world community to respect the right of the people of Karabakh to guard their security, though they noticed the lack of security in the initiative." Snark News Agency, Yerevan, May 27, 1993, in FBIS-SOV-93-102, 5-28-93, p. 56. While Armenia accepted the plan, it drew attention to the security concerns of the Karabakh Armenians.

In December 1994, the Karabakh parliament elected Robert Kocharian president for two years, with the right to appoint the prime minister. After that, elections will be held for a president having a five year term.

[76]Migdalovitz, p. 5.

[77]Konstantin Eggert, "Stepanakert idet na vstrechu trebovaniyam mezhdunarodnogo soobshchestva," *Izvestiya*, Moscow, June 16, 1993, p.3 and Sergei Bablumyan, "Rukovodstvo Nagornogo Karabakha odobrilo initsiativu SBSE," *Izvestiya*, Moscow, June 16, 1993, p. 1.

[78]Huseinov, a thirty-four-year-old militia commander and national war hero, was the former head of a textile concern in Yevlakh in northeast Azerbaijan. With money he made from the mill and from various dealings, some reported to be illegal, Huseinov outfitted and equipped a private militia that was instrumental in recapturing Mardakert province in the second half of 1992. He was relieved of his command after a series of military defeats in February 1993 and was ordered back to Baku. He refused the order and remained commander of the 709th Brigade of the Azerbaijani Army based in Ganje, Azerbaijan's second-largest city. Reportedly, he maintained excellent contacts with the Russian 104th Airborne division, also based in Ganje; furthermore, part of Huseinov's unit was housed on the 104th Airborne division's base.

Quick to exploit the power vacuum in Baku, in July Karabakh Armenian forces seized Agdam, a city of 50,000 lying about six kilometers from Nagorno-Karabakh's eastern border. During heavy fighting that lasted over a month, Karabakh Armenian military units first encircled Agdam, finally capturing the city on July 23, 1993. During their offensive against Agdam, Karabakh Armenian forces committed several violations of the rules of war, including hostage-taking, indiscriminate fire, and the forcible displacement of civilians. After the city was captured, it was intentionally looted and burned under orders of Karabakh Armenian authorities, another serious violation of the rules of war.[79]

After confused fighting on June 4, in which between 20-70 people lost their lives, Huseinov then demanded the resignation of President Elchibey and the Popular Front Government. (There are reports that most of those killed were government soldiers ambushed by Huseinov's men as they left Ganje). With a small rag tag force, he began his largely unopposed march on Baku.

On June 18, President Elchibey fled the capital and returned to his native village of Keleki in the Nakhichevan enclave. Nine days later, Huseinov arrived in Baku, where he was greeted by Heidar Aliyev, who had been elected chairman of Azerbaijan's parliament two weeks earlier. After three days of horse trading, Huseinov was named prime minister with responsibility for the "power ministries": defense, internal affairs, and national security.

A crackdown on the press and the Popular Front began. With scant protest, Western governments accepted Elchibey's overthrow. In October 1993, Heidar Aliyev was elected President, a post he holds to this day. Huseinov, however, was removed from power and charged with treason after an alleged coup attempt in October 1994.

Many commentators saw Moscow's work in Surat Huseinov's overthrow of Elchibey's pro-Turkish Popular Front Government. Thomas Goltz, a Baku-based journalist and commentator, develops this theme in a thoughtful essay, "Letter from Eurasia: The Hidden Russian Hand," *Foreign Policy*, Fall 1993.

Azerbaijan under Popular Front rule was defiantly anti-Russian, refusing to join the CIS and demanding the complete withdrawal of all Russian forces from its territory. The last Russian unit, the above-mentioned 104th Airborne Division in Ganje, pulled out of Azerbaijan on May 28, 1993 making Azerbaijan the only former Soviet republic without Russian troops in its territory. While the soldiers of the 104th Airborne left, most of their weapons did not, falling to Huseinov and his troops. According to Goltz, this precipitated the coup.

While President Aliyev brought Azerbaijan into the CIS fold, he continues to refuse to allow any substantial Russian military presence in Azerbaijan, including peacekeepers.

[79]A month earlier, on June 28, 1993, Karabakh Armenian forces captured Mardakert, the last Azeri-held stronghold in Nagorno-Karabakh. Before the war, the mostly Armenian-populated city was Karabakh's second largest.

Reflecting the tit-for-tat nature of the conflict, in Agdam Armenian forces took revenge for the Azeri destruction of Mardakert. Thomas Goltz, who was in Mardakert in September 1992 while the city was still under Azeri control, made the following observation: "The city of Mardakert...is now a pile of rubble. After the burned houses and smashed vehicles, the eye is drawn to the more intimate detritus of destroyed private lives: pots and pans, suitcases leaking sullied clothes, crushed baby strollers and even family portraits, still in shattered frames."

Situated about thirty kilometers northeast of Stepanakert just over Karabakh's border with Azerbaijan, Agdam had been on the conflict's front line. Karabakh Armenian forces considered Agdam a main staging area for Azeri attacks against their Nagorno-Karabakh enclave.[80] Artillery duels across the border were common in 1992: Azeri artillery would bombard Askeran[81] and Stepanakert, while Karabakh Armenian forces would return the favor by shelling Agdam and the villages that surrounded it.[82] This use of imprecisely aimed artillery at population centers was indiscriminate, in violation of the rules of war.[83]

Kemal, a sixty-nine-year-old electrician who lived in Agdam until its capture by Karabakh Armenians, describes years marked by war. During one intensive period of shelling in 1993, several of his neighbors were killed:

> Missiles and shells had already fallen on the town for a couple of years. Both sides would fire at each other. There was an Azeri artillery unit maybe a kilometer from our home; heavy fighting and shelling had been happening in and around Agdam since the beginning of 1993. My sons — I have three — were at the front in the self-defense forces. During this period shells would fall on the town almost everyday. When it became too much, we would evacuate the women and children about two or three kilometers away to suburbs not under such bombardment. Sometimes this happened twice in the same day. Once, a Grad missile hit the house of my neighbor Hassan. He lived about one hundred meters from me. He was sitting in the yard. The missile killed him, an old

---

In TCG-33, Institute of Current World Affairs, Hanover, New Hampshire, September 18, 1992.

[80]Azerbaijani authorities branded Stepanakert "the main nest of the enemy." See, Paul Quinn-Judge, "200 Reported Dead in Armenian-Azeri Clashes," *Boston Globe*, March 8, 1992.

[81]Askeran is an ethnic Armenian city in Karabakh about seven kilometers from Agdam. During a brief half hour visit to Askeran that Karabakh Armenian authorities allowed us in April 1994, we observed the remains of heavy shell damage.

[82]*See* Human Rights Watch/Helsinki's 1992 *Escalation of the Armed Conflict in Nagorno-Karabakh* for a more detailed description of fighting in the area and damage to civilian objects in 1992.
Stepanakert also was mercilessly bombarded from Shusha, an Azeri-populated city about five kilometers south-west of the city. On March 12, for example, 140 rockets fell on the city. See Paul Quinn-Judge, "Death, Fear in Armenian Enclave," *Boston Globe*, March 13, 1992, p. 2.

[83]*See* Appendix A, International Law.

woman, and three young children. I helped take the bodies to the mosque and to the cemetery. I don't know what they were shooting at because there wasn't anything connected with the army around us.[84]

By June 1993, the initiative had long passed to Karabakh Armenian forces. On June 12, 1993, with Surat Huseinov's rebellion barely a week old, Karabakh Armenian forces launched their main offensive east towards Agdam.[85] They moved in a large, encircling movement: two pincers of Grad fire, heavy artillery, and tanks slowly working their way around Agdam from the north and south. In the north they first seized Farukh mountain, a height commanding Agdam about ten kilometers to the northeast. Next came Khidirli, a village around which units of the Azerbaijani army had taken up positions.

Qiyasli, about three kilometers east of Khidirli, was shelled on June 20, from the direction of the Karabakh town of Khanabad (ten kilometers to the southwest), according to Gonul, whose family worked on the Dzerzhinskii Collective farm in the village. The shelling continued and on June 22, Gonul was wounded by indiscriminate fire and her home damaged:

It was about 11:00 A.M. I was in the courtyard of our house, cleaning rice and preparing for lunch. Suddenly, three shells hit. The first exploded by the gate and sprayed a tractor with shrapnel, about twenty meters away. The second one hit behind the house. The third, unfortunately, was a direct hit on the house. The explosion collapsed the roof and some walls and knocked me down. I tried to get up, but collapsed. Then I realized I was covered in blood. I could see smoke. My husband was at work, so I starting shouting for my son.[86]

Her son, who was serving in the Azerbaijani army in a unit stationed at Khidirli, ran back to Qiyasli village the day his mother was wounded as his unit's situation became hopeless, and he saw Qiyasli burning. En route, the son saw the bodies of several civilians killed by indiscriminate and targeted Karabakh Armenian

---

[84]Interview, Refugee Camp, Saatli, March 30, 1994.

[85]Baku Azertac, June 13, 1993, in FBIS-SOV-93-112, June 14, 1993, p. 79; "Azerbaijan Says Armenians are Gaining Ground in Heavy Fighting," *The New York Times*, June 13, 1993.
    At the time both the Armenian government in Yerevan and the Armenian authorities in Karabakh denied that an offensive was taking place. The Karabakh Armenians admitted only "defensive action". Eyewitness accounts, however, clearly refute their denials.

[86]Interview, Barda, Azerbaijan, March 31, 1994.

fire:

> As I made my way towards my home in Qiyasli, I saw several dead and wounded civilians along the road. Two I knew by sight: Elshan, about thirty, and Surhai, maybe fifty. They came from the next village over to the east, Etyemezli, to try and help evacuate people. A bullet had struck Elshan in the head; his body was still lying on the ground, fully clothed. Etibar, who was with Elshan, said [Karabakh] Armenian troops fired on them as they approached. Etibar managed to escape and hide. He told me the [Karabakh] Armenians then stole the car. I saw Surhai in the vineyard. He was dead, but I can't tell you how. I finally reached home and saw my mother lying on the ground, all bloody and screaming. I picked her up and gave her water. I put my mother in our car and we fled north towards Barda. By that time I had stopped at my brother's house to get out of my uniform. I didn't want people to think that I was a deserter. We headed north along the Agdam-Barda road, but some [Karabakh] Armenian tanks were ahead of us. Then the [Karabakh] Armenian soldiers starting shooting at us. We managed to escape, others did not. It was a mess.[87]

In the confusion, some Azeri civilians entered battle areas unaware that they had fallen to Karabakh Armenian units. By June 23, it seems Karabakh Armenian units passed east of Qiyasli and were already several kilometers behind Agdam to the east, near the small village of Sajali. Azeri civilians were either pushed out or taken hostage.

The Pashayev family lived in Sajali. They left on June 20 to visit relatives in Baku, when no fighting was taking place. On June 22, about 7:00 P.M., the six members of the Pashayev family returning home were fired on by Karabakh Armenian forces and taken hostage in Sajali:

> It was well after midnight when we approached Qaradagli, the village next to ours. There were some Azeri soldiers in Qaradagli. We asked them what the situation was like, and they told us that the [Karabakh] Armenians were still in the vicinity of Agdam and had not reached this far east. They said our village, Sajali, was unoccupied, so we proceeded on. There was no shooting as we entered Sajali, and no one tried to warn us. All of a sudden, people started to shoot at us. The next thing I realized the car had stopped.

---

[87]Interview, Barda, Azerbaijan, March 31, 1994.

> Almost immediately several [Karabakh] Armenian soldiers
> approached our car. They shouted at us, "Why have you come
> here? Didn't you know we took this place." My father, Mujat, died
> instantly. They then took my husband away. I and my two sons
> were wounded, so the Karabakh Armenian soldiers bandaged us.
> It didn't save my nine- year-old son, Nevjat, who died while we
> were still in the village. A truck came about two hours after the
> attack, about five in the morning. My mother stayed in the village.[88]

This woman had serious bullet wounds to both legs and one of her arms;
another of her sons had an arm wound. They were taken by Karabakh Armenian forces
to the Stepanakert hospital. According to her, "At first they wanted to amputate my
son's arm. I cried and asked them not to, to think of his future. Then the Armenian
surgeon, Dr. Edik Stepanian, looked at me and said, 'I'll do everything I can to save his
arm. It could be my own child, and I'll think of him as that.'" Her son's arm was saved.
After about a week she and her son were exchanged for hostages held by the Azeris.
Her husband, Khagani, a young man of thirty-three, was not so lucky and remains a
hostage in Nagorno-Karabakh, reportedly in the Shusha prison.

Karabakh Armenian forces also moved south of Agdam to encircle the city.
On the morning of June 12, they entered the villages of Merzili and Yusufjanli, about
seven kilometers southeast of Agdam.[89] There Karabakh Armenian forces killed
civilians, took hostages, and destroyed civilian dwellings. Kerim, age thirty, a worker
at a state collective farm near Yusufjanli, a village of 600 houses, remembers the day
well, as it was the last time he saw his father.

> My house was about 500 meters from the home of my parents, Ali-
> aga and Kekli. Both of them are fifty-five. I saw my father at about
> 8:30 or 9:00 A.M. on the morning of June 12. He told me that the
> [Karabakh] Armenians had taken the village of Giyamadin, which
> is right next to ours. We knew we had to leave. I went back home,
> got my family and headed out of the village.[90]

Kerim reached the outskirts of Yusufjanli, about one kilometer from his
home, maybe an hour later at 10:00 A.M. He waited for his parents, but they did not
arrive; they were robbed and captured by Karabakh Armenians.

We could see smoke coming from the village when we were

---

[88]Interview, Baku, Azerbaijan, March 28, 1994.

[89]Baku Turan News Agency, June 12, 1993, in FBIS-SOV-93-112, June 14, 1993, p. 79.

[90]Interview, displaced persons camp, Barda, Azerbaijan, March 31, 1994.

waiting. One could also hear rifle fire. I began to worry because
my parents still hadn't come. I knew I had to go back and look for
them, but the road was too dangerous so I went alone by foot
through the vineyards. I reached the village, and lay down at the
edge of the vineyard and hid myself. I was maybe thirty meters
away and could see about twelve [Karabakh] Armenian soldiers
and a BMP.[91] Then a tractor came rumbling along. A couple of the
[Karabakh] Armenian soldiers opened fire on it. They then went up
to the tractor and pulled out what I saw was my mother and father.
They yanked two rings off her and pushed both my mother and
father in the back of the BMP. They then looted what was on the
tractor and shot the hell out of it. They then all got in the BMP and
drove off.[92]

Several hours later that day, the Karabakh Armenian forces withdrew from
Yusufjanli.[93] Several of the village men — including Kerim, Ali, and Zaman — plus
some Azeri soldiers entered the village one last time. Five Azeri civilians lay where
they were killed. Dead animals littered the ground, houses burned and smoldered.
According to Kerim,

Peri Jafarova, an old woman, age eighty, and her granddaughter,
Melahat Akhmedova, maybe twenty, were in the road shot down.
The old woman couldn't run fast enough. Farther on I saw Gasham
Gambarov dead on the ground with a bullet to his head, surrounded
by his livestock, just as dead. Sukur Nejefi, thirty-four, was killed
in front of his house in his car, a red Lada. It looked as if a tank or
something had rolled over it. His sister, Fiza Allahverdi, thirty-
seven, was lying with her stomach shot open in the doorway of the
house.

Ali, who also saw these dead bodies, returned to a gutted home; "it was
strange because nobody took anything. They just burned the house with everything in
it."[94] Zaman, fifty-six, found the same thing when he returned to his house. "When I left

---

[91]A BMP is a Soviet-made armored personnel carrier.

[92]Interview, displaced persons camp, Barda, Azerbaijan, April 1, 1994.

[93]Baku Turan News Agency, 12 June 1993, in FBIS-SOV-93-112, June 14 1993. Turan
reported that units of the Azeri army re-took the villages. The men with whom we spoke said
the Armenians withdrew.

[94]Interview, displaced persons camp, Barda, Azerbaijan, April 1, 1994.

at 10:00 A.M. that morning everything was fine in the house. I returned six hours later to a smoldering mess. The roof had collapsed into the house; I could see the roof tiles through the windows." According to the men, about 60 percent of the village suffered such damage.

While the men of Yusufjanli were spending their last day in the burnt-out village, Kekli and her husband, Ali Aga, were locked in a BMP on their way to the Karabakh town of Martuni to begin their first day as hostages. Kekli reported that she was beaten and her gold teeth were pulled, without benefit of anesthesia:

> They took us out of the BMP in front of what I think was the police
> station. Some [Karabakh] Armenian women saw us and started to
> scream, "Give us back our sons." My husband and I were locked in
> a room with Mirza Rizayev, who is from our village of Yusufjanli,
> a soldier from Merzili, and a soldier from Saidli. They beat us all.
> Later, it was already dark, a guard called me out and brought me to
> a room. I was held down and my gold teeth — twelve — were
> pulled out with a pliers. They didn't give my anything for the pain,
> but my face was already swollen from the beating so I didn't feel
> the full effect. Later they did the same thing to my husband.

Two days later, Kekli was separated from her husband and taken to the house of a woman in Martuni whose son, a Karabakh Armenian soldier, had died fighting near Merzili village. The woman wanted the body of her son back and hoped to trade Kekli for it.

Kekli stayed at the woman's house for about two weeks, where she ate with the family. When the body of the woman's son was found, negotiations were started on her release. She was moved back to Martuni, to the home of another family member. Her treatment here was good.

She was exchanged for a corpse on July 1, 1993 outside of Merzili village, Agdam Province. Her husband is still a hostage in Martuni.[95] The taking of hostages and the torture or inhuman treatment of captives are grave breaches of the Geneva Conventions.[96]

The battle for Agdam raged on into July. On June 30, Col. Surat Huseinov announced that he would personally lead his troops into battle and supposedly headed for the front, but there are reports that Huseinov did little to resupply or reinforce

---

[95]The exchange was an *ad hoc*, battlefield swap. Local commanders on both sides declared an impromptu cease-fire and exchanged Kekli for the corpse.

[96]IV Geneva, article 147. See Appendix A, International Law.

Agdam, considered an Elchibey stronghold.[97] General mobilization was declared a few days later, but with little effect.[98] By July 5, the city was virtually surrounded by the Karabakh Armenians and under heavy bombardment from artillery and Grad missile fire.[99] Only one road was open out of Agdam, and that was crowded with Azeris fleeing east in anything capable of movement: cars, trucks, tractors pulling sledges, and horse carts.[100] Smoke rose from the occupied villages around Agdam. An Azeri counteroffensive managed to re-take a few villages, but what really delayed the fall of Agdam was former Minsk Group Chairman Mario Raffaelli's ill-fated visit to the region from July 9-15, 1993.[101] Fighting broke out again almost immediately after his departure from the area, and Agdam fell on July 23, 1993.

Aleksandr, an eighty-two-year-old Don Cossack and invalid from the Second World War, was still in Agdam when it fell. He had lived in Azerbaijan since 1929. Aleksandr has the following memory of July 23, 1993, the day Karabakh Armenian troops entered Agdam, robbed him, and took him hostage:

> I was at home, I'm rather sickly. I was in the kitchen boiling some tea when [there was an explosion] and glass flew all over the kitchen. . . . I was already used to it, firing and firing, without end — sometimes from here, sometimes from there. . . . Most people who had cars had already left. . . . I ran [to the window] and saw the sidewalk. There were [Karabakh] Armenian soldiers along the sidewalk, maybe twenty or twenty-five, with their guns trained all over our apartment building. They thought there were soldiers here. Then they opened up. I tried to hide in the corner. . . my hands were all bloody from the glass. I turned to run and I got a small piece of shrapnel in the back.[102]

---

[97] June 29, 1993, Moscow Radio, Moscow World Service, in FBIS-SOV-93-124, June 30, 1993, p. 70.

[98] John Auerbach, "Armenia force nears key Azerbaijan town," *Boston Globe*, July 6, 1993, p. 2.

[99] Sokhbet Mamedov, "Oppozitsiya vystupayet v zashchitu El'chibeya, a v osazhdennom Agdame polykhayet pozhar," *Izvestiya*, Moscow, July 7, 1993, p.2.

[100] "2 Caucasus Regions Sinking Deeper into Civil War," *The New York Times*, July 6, 1993.

[101] Migdalovitz, p. 7.

[102] Interview, Baku, Azerbaijan, March 28, 1994.

Several soldiers started searching Aleksandr's apartment building floor by floor. When they reached his apartment, they broke the door down with their rifle butts and entered.

> They shouted at me "Hands up" and "Get out." Then they started demanding money. I had 14,000 rubles, so I gave it to them. . . . One took me into the kitchen and started to demand gold. "Give me the gold, give me the gold," he shouted. I didn't have any gold, so he took my military medals off, put them in his pocket laughing, and left. The others then took me hostage.[103]

Aleksandr was held hostage in Agdam, in Yerevan, Armenia, and in Stepanakert, Nagorno-Karabakh, until his release through the ICRC[104] in February 1994. He reported that his conditions of captivity were acceptable, though food was sometimes inadequate. In Yerevan, Armenia's capital, where he was held at the Home for the Aged Number One, he stayed with Armenians, including some Armenian refugees from Baku. All received the same rations.

Over the next several weeks, Karabakh forces systematically and methodically looted and burned Agdam and the villages surrounding it. According to witnesses, smoke rising from the Agdam area during August 1993 was visible for ten to twenty miles. A journalist in the village of Baghbanlar, south of Agdam, observed, "A soldier strutted out of a house carrying a porcelain sink and a wrench in one hand, while another filled the sidecar of his motorcycle with the contents of someone's garage. A tanker truck wheeled into town and headed for the wine and cognac factory."[105]

A Western diplomat active in the OSCE Minsk Group talks said that the burning and looting of Agdam was not the result of undisciplined troops, but was a well-orchestrated plan organized by Karabakh authorities in Stepanakert.[106]

---

[103]It is common for Soviet veterans of the Second World War to wear their decorations on their civilian clothes.

[104]The ICRC has facilitated release of hostages and prisoners of war by physically accomplishing the exchanges, but does not negotiate any exchanges.

[105]Raymond Bonner, "War in Caucasus Shows Ethnic Hate's Front Line," *The New York Times,* August 2, 1993, p. 6.

[106]The Karabakh Armenians run their state in a highly organized, highly centralized manner. For instance, unlike Armenia, where black marketeers peddle gas every few hundred meters along the road, gasoline is not sold in Nagorno-Karabakh; rather, it is rationed out by central military authorities. Thus the gas and transport needed to undertake the looting of a city of 50,000 could only be obtained through the Karabakh authorities.

Extensive destruction and appropriation of property, not justified by military necessity and carried out unlawfully and wantonly, is a grave breach of the Geneva Conventions.

U.N. SECURITY COUNCIL RESOLUTION 853

Several short-lived and ill-fated peace attempts followed the July 23 capture of Agdam. On July 25, an erratically observed cease-fire was announced by Karabakh Armenian authorities and the Azerbaijani government.

Four days later, on July 29, the U.N. Security Council passed Resolution 853 based on a report by the former OSCE Minsk Group Chairman Mario Raffaelli. The resolution condemned the seizure of Agdam, called on all parties to cease supplying weapons that could "lead to the intensification of the conflict or the continued occupation of territory," and called on the Republic of Armenia to use its "influence" with the Karabakh authorities to bring about their compliance with all U.N. resolutions and Minsk Group initiatives. The resolution also called for the lifting of all economic and energy blockades in the region.[107] Resolution 853 was a clear censure of the Karabakh Armenians' recent military actions.

While the Azerbaijani government applauded the resolution, the Karabakh Armenians did not.[108] They thought it was biased because it was based on the July 27 report of Raffaelli, whom they charged with favoring Azerbaijan in the conflict.[109] In an appeal to Raffaelli on August 4, Karen Baburyan, acting chairman of the Nagorno-Karabakh parliament, accused the OSCE Minsk Group of unilaterally branding Karabakh the aggressor, while ignoring Azerbaijani transgressions: "The Republic of Nagorno-Karabakh doesn't pretend to capture strange territories but when guns fire on Karabakh towns and villages we have to neutralize them. We have no other way

---

[107]United Nations Security Council, Resolution 853, 29 July 1993, S/RES/853/ (1993).

[108]Sokhbet Mamedov, "Sovet Bezopasnosti OON osudil okkupatsiyu azerbaidzhanskikh territorii," *Izvestiya*, Moscow, August 3, 1993, p.1.
While the government of the Republic of Armenia accepted most of U.N. Security Council Resolution 853, it hoped that "the international community, comprehending the threat to the lives and security of the people of Nagorno Karabakh, will demonstrate a more balanced position on these issues." Statement, Ministry of Foreign Affairs of the Republic of Armenia, August 2, 1993.

[109]"Peremiriye Prodleno, diplomaticheskiye srazheniya prodolzhayutsya," *Russkaya Mysl'*, Paris, August 5, 1993, p. 5.
Reportedly, the Karabakh Armenians were angered by Raffaelli's sharp criticism of their seizure of Agdam as well as by his addressing them as "the Armenian community of Nagorno-Karabakh." According to the author of the article, it had been the practice in OSCE documents to refer to the Karabakh Armenians as the "elected officials of Nagorno-Karabakh."

out."[110]

KARABAKH ARMENIAN FORCES PUSH TOWARDS THE IRANIAN BORDER-AUGUST 1993

Over the next three months, in two stages, Karabakh Armenian forces — with the reported support of Armenian forces — pushed south out of their mountain enclave all the way to the Araks river, Azerbaijan's border with Iran.[111] During August-October 1993, the Karabakh Armenians seized four new Azerbaijani provinces: Qubatli, Jebrayil, Fizuli, and Zangelan, which had a combined population of between 250,000 and 300,000.[112] During their two-stage offensive, Karabakh Armenian forces committed several violations of the rules of war, including forced displacement of the civilian population, indiscriminate fire, hostage-taking, and the looting and destruction of civilian objects.

Again Karabakh Armenian forces justified the action by the need to stop hostile artillery fire originating from these provinces. Again several hundred thousand new Azeri civilians became displaced persons or refugees, with some seeking

---

[110]Yerevan Snark News Agency, August 4, 1993, in FBIS-SOV-93-151, August 9, 1993, p. 65.

[111]While Armenians fought to capture four new Azerbaijani provinces, Heidar Aliyev fought for power in Baku and consolidated his hold. He cracked down on the press and the political opposition, acting quickly to legitimize the coup that brought him to power. While President Elchibey, reportedly suffering from depression, fled Baku for the safety of his native Keleki village in Nakhichevan, he did not formally renounce the presidency. In mid-July, Elchibey even renounced his decision of June 24, 1993 temporarily transferring the power of his office to the chairman of the Azerbaijani Supreme Soviet, Heidar Aliyev.

On August 29, 1993, Aliyev held a vote of confidence on the rule of President Elchibey. Aliyev stated that, "the president [Elchibey], who fled his post and does not carry out his duties at such a hard time for the country, should not be the head of state." Widespread discontent at Elchibey's Popular Front government and the popular belief that Elchibey was personally responsible for the events of June 1993 brought Aliyev a resounding victory.

A little over a month later, on October 3, 1993, in new presidential elections, Heidar Aliyev received 98.8 percent of the vote against two other opponents. The elections were far from free: the major political parties were not allowed to field candidates, and the media was strictly controlled.

[112]These provinces are located south of Nagorno-Karabakh, wedged between it and the Iranian border (the Araks River), in a strip of land between fifteen to thirty-five kilometers wide. With the exception of Zangelan, they all share a border with Nagorno-Karabakh. They run from east to west in the following order: Fizuli, Jebrayil, Qubatli, and Zangelan. Qubatli is south of Lachin province; Zangelan is south of Qubatli. The main provincial city gives each province its name.

temporary shelter in Iran.

While the Azerbaijani army fought for Agdam, it offered little resistance to this southern thrust before collapsing into an unorganized, mass retreat. A western diplomat who toured the region in August termed the Azerbaijani defenses "nil"; "It is not a matter of whether the Armenians can take the region, but when."[113] By the end of August, Fizuli, Qubatli, and Jebrayil cities had fallen and tens of thousands of civilians were displaced, pressed in a thin strip of land against the Iranian border.

Serious fighting had been going on along Karabakh's southern border with Azerbaijan since April 1993, when Karabakh Armenian forces launched an offensive against Qubatli and Fizuli provinces. During the August 1993 Karabakh Armenian offensive, there were several reports of involvement by troops from the Republic of Armenia. These forces reportedly committed serious human rights abuses. On July 25, the date of the cease-fire after the fall of Agdam, the city of Fizuli became the front line. By August 9, heavy fighting had erupted all along the southern front.[114] Both sides accused each other of breaking the cease-fire. Fizuli was surrounded by Karabakh Armenian forces, and the city fell on August 20.

Karabakh Armenian forces killed several Azeri civilians who were trying to flee, shooting into towns and villages even after Azeri soldiers had fled and no resistance to their advance was offered. On the day that Fizuli fell, Sumaya, age forty-six, fled her home in Merdini village, ten kilometers east of Fizuli,[115] as her brother-in-law was killed by Karabakh Armenian forces.

That morning, Azerbaijani soldiers warned her to flee, though she and her neighbors did not. Then around 2:00 P.M. Grad rockets started to fall near the village, shaking the walls and breaking the windows of her home. Several hours later, retreating Azeri soldiers fled through the village, saying that they could no longer hold off the Karabakh Armenians. Then the Karabakh Armenian troops arrived. According to Sumaya, her brother-in-law died when his car was hit by fire from Karabakh Armenian forces as he was trying to escape:

> At around 6:00 P.M. that night, after the Azerbaijani soldiers ran
> through our village, we saw [Karabakh] Armenian tanks and BTRs
> approach Merdini. The people that were left broke into a panic —
> everyone went for his car, truck, tractor, anything to escape. There
> was shooting. My family got in one car, my brother-in-law,
> Pehlavan Aliyev, in another behind our car. A third vehicle was in

---

[113]"Caucasus City Falls to Armenian Forces," *The New York Times*, August 24, 1993, p. a7.

[114]"Fighting Around Nagorno-Karabakh," U.S. State Department statement, Washington, D.C., August 9, 1993.

[115]According to Sumaya, the village consists of about 150 houses and is situated between the larger villages of Qarakhanbeyli and Alkhanli.

front of us. We raced out the small road towards the main asphalt road that leads to Ahmedbeyli, about twenty kilometers from Merdini near the Iranian border. We had just turned onto this main road when suddenly there was smoke behind us where my brother-in-law had been. We couldn't stop for him, we just kept on driving.[116]

Later that day there was a localized Azeri counterattack, and some Azeri soldiers found Pehlavan Aliyev. Sumaya saw him again at a hospital in Beilagan: "He had injuries and burns on his leg, head, left arm. One of his eyes had been blown out. He told me that a round or something had hit his car. He died later, and we buried him in Beilagan."

On August 23, Karabakh Armenian forces took the village of Hovostu, a settlement of some 250 houses fifteen kilometers north of the Araks River in Jebrayil province. According to Mr. N., Azeri forces had taken up positions in trenches outside the village but had abandoned them on the arrival of Karabakh Armenian forces. The Karabakh Armenians continued their practice of shooting at villages where they encountered no resistance in order to force the civilian population to flee. Those forces killed several civilians, among them four relatives of this witness:

Around 1:00 or 2:00 P.M. we saw [Karabakh] Armenian tanks outside the village. The Azeri soldiers just fled, they didn't have a chance. They were very poorly equipped. Then the [Karabakh] Armenians started to shoot at us [civilians], and a panic broke out. We just left everything and fled. They were shooting as we ran. I saw bodies everywhere as we ran out of the village. I saw the dead bodies of four of my relatives: Nanakhanim Peraliyeva, a woman of about sixty; Narkhanim Mamedova, a few years younger than her; Hajikhanim Mamedova, a woman in her early thirties; and Makhnise Amarakhova, forty-five. They were all bloody, lying on ground.[117]

They reached the Araks river, where they had to wait two days before crossing on August 25. They crossed on makeshift rafts and ropes. When they reached the other side, Iranian officials were waiting and assisted them.

Forces — reported to be from the Republic of Armenia — also moved west of Jebrayil that August, south along the Akera river in the direction of Qubatli. Micheal Tschanz, an ICRC official in the area at the time, reported the presence of troops from the Republic of Armenia in neighboring Zangelan province: "The Azeris

---

[116]Interview, displaced persons camp, Agjabedi, Azerbaijan, April 1, 1994.

[117]Interview, displaced persons camp, Saatli, Azerbaijan, March 30, 1994.

are fighting on two fronts. . . . According to our information, Armenians from Armenia have crossed the border and occupied some villages in Zangelan province."[118]

On August 28, 1993, Armenian forces reached the village of Qarakishiler, about ten kilometers northeast of Qubatli. Sixty-one-year-old Fakrat was taken hostage and beaten by soldiers he believed had come from Kafan, in the Republic of Armenia, not from Nagorno-Karabakh:

> Armenian troops surrounded our village [Qarakisiler] at about 3:00 P.M. on August 28. There was some shooting, and then they simply came in and took hostage whomever was left. There were four in my group when they captured us: Elekhbir Elekhbirov, Idris Akhmedov, Abdulla Agayev, and myself. They hit us with their fists and with rifle butts and screamed, "Let's go, faster!"[119]

The four hostages were then taken to Gazidere, about fifteen miles north of Qarakishiler near the Armenian border. At Gazidere, the headquarters of this military unit. the beating continued. "The commander, his name was Ashot, told the men not to beat me because I'm old. But it was a free-for-all with the other three. They were all bloody, stumbling on the ground from the blows." Fakrat reported.

Fakrat spent the next two months in prisons in Sisian and Kafan in the Republic of Armenia. While food was poor, he did receive medicine for his diabetes. He was exchanged on November 15, 1993.

Four days after Armenian forces captured Qarakishiler, on Wednesday, September 1, the Azerbaijani Defense Ministry reported that its forces had abandoned the town of Qubatli under heavy pressure.[120]

On August 31, Karabakh Armenian forces reached Chaitumas, a small settlement about ten kilometers south of Qarakishiler, on the Akera river. By then Karabakh Armenian forces advanced within twenty kilometers of the Iranian border. They continued to take hostage those who were unable to flee, mostly the elderly and infirm. Rovshan, over sixty, lived in a nearby village with his wife Leyla.[121] Unlike

---

[118]"Azerbaijan Claims Armenians Seized Key Town." *The New York Times*. September 5, 1993, p. 19.

[119]Interview, Baku, Azerbaijan, March 28, 1993. Fakrat said he had traveled often to Kafan during peacetime and could tell from the accents of his captors when they spoke Armenian that they were not Karabakh Armenians, but from Kafan or Sisian.

[120]Karabakh forces claimed that Azerbaijani units abandoned the town on August 31. Reuters. "Azeri Army withdraws from Town." September 2, 1993.

[121]This is a pseudonym. The witness did not want his name used because he fears for his wife. who is still in Armenian captivity.

most of their neighbors, they stayed when the attack came because Leyla was ill. Rovshan was taken hostage, beaten, and forced to work by his captors:

> The [Karabakh] Armenians came on August 31. My wife could not be moved, so we couldn't flee. We stayed in our house until September 4, 1993. During that time the [Karabakh] Armenians looted the houses and drove away most of the livestock north, towards the village of Ishygly. On September 4, the commander of a battalion in Martuni, in Nagorno-Karabakh, — I think they called him Mavoh — came to our house with his daughter. He said, "Your wife will stay here, but you will come with us." That's the last time I saw her. I did odd jobs when I was in Martuni — sweeping up, helping chop wood. . . . I was beaten a lot there by soldiers. They would stand on my ankles, knock me down.[122]

Rovshan was eventually transferred to Shusha. He and some other Azerbaijani hostages were exchanged in late 1993 for a Karabakh Armenian captive. His wife is still captive but her whereabouts are unknown.

HG, age eighty-one, not only was taken hostage and beaten, but also witnessed the gang rape of two Azeri woman by Armenian soldiers.[123] He was captured in Hoje[124] as he fled with a group of Azeri civilians on August 30, 1993, from the advancing Armenians. In his group were four men, an older woman of forty-five, and a young woman carrying her two-day-old dead infant in her arms. The infant had died in the hospital and the family was in the process of burying the infant when the attack started; they fled with the body. The women were from Hoje.

Mr. G, who had served in the Soviet Army in World War II, was sure that the captors were from an Armenian battalion which included about 200 troops, five tanks, and two armored personnel carriers. All the troops wore the same uniform; they even told him they were from the Armenian army.

The captives were held in Hoje, during which time Mr. G saw several big trucks enter and rob twelve to fifteen of the sixty houses in Hoje; he could not see the rest of the houses. They were held two days in Tartumaj village of Jebrayil, where the men were beaten but not interrogated. Tartumaj was burned down when they arrived. Only two public buildings used to house the battalion were still standing. The captives were held in a wooden shack like those used to store wine. It had a dirt floor and nothing to sleep on. While in this shack, they were fed once in two days.

---

[122]Interview, Baku, Azerbaijan, April 4, 1994.

[123]Interview, Baku, Azerbaijan, March 28, 1994.

[124]Although he lived in Milani, a village on a hill in Qubatli province, he and others fled to Hoje, twenty kilometers away, when Milani was attacked seven days earlier.

The old man cried as he told Human Rights Watch/Helsinki that the two women captives were raped before the eyes of the male captives. The off-duty soldiers and officers[125] came into the room where all the captives were held and raped the women two or three times a day. The attackers did not pay attention to the shouting or cries of the women, nor to the pleas made on behalf of the young woman, age twenty-two, who had just delivered and then lost her first-born child a few days earlier.

The captives were then taken by truck to Martuni in southeastern Karabakh. They were held in a police prison. The men and women were separated at this point, and the men taken to a cell where there were other Azeri captives, fifteen men in all. Some were soldiers captured on the Beilagan front, and they received the most severe beatings, sometimes from young Armenian drunks who entered the cell three or four times to taunt and beat the prisoners. The guards occasionally intervened but they were also afraid.

In Martuni, where he was held for a month, the approximately thirty prisoners he saw there were given scant rations. This eighty-one-year-old man was forced, under guard, to sweep the streets and clean out the yards and livestock pens of private persons in Martuni, as well as warehouses. He worked long hours, from morning till dark. The prisoners were interrogated in Martuni by their guards and visited by the ICRC.

He and some other prisoners were called out of the cell in late September and sent to Shusha for six days. En route and in Shusha, they were taunted by Karabakh Armenians, who among other things demanded that they sing Azeri songs and would beat them when they said they did not know the songs.

In Shusha there were about six Azeri men in jail. There they were not beaten and received better food. He was held in Shusha for six days, where the men were again forced to work under guard: the young had to cut wood and the older men were put to work digging.

In Shusha, two men from the "Armenian Committee" interrogated him about his name, age, family names and addresses, and whether he had sons in the army. He understood they were doing this for hostage exchange purposes.

Then he was sent to Kafan in Armenia, where he was held with three other Azeris and interviewed by the chief of police of Kafan, also about his family and the number of his children. He was held in an Armenian jail in Kafan for fourteen days, during which time he was not beaten or required to work, but was given food only once a day.

He was exchanged for three Armenian corpses: a major, a surgeon, and a soldier, on October 18, 1993.[126]

Seli, sixty-four, lived in Mahrouz, a village close to Khanlik where a small bridge crosses the Akera river. Largely agricultural, the Khanlik area is dotted with

---

[125]On the officers' uniforms were stars denoting rank.

[126]Interview, Baku, Azerbaijan, March 28, 1993.

collective farms. Seli witnessed several attacks on Mahrouz in the last week in August that left scores of civilians dead and wounded.[127]

According to Seli, Karabakh Armenian forces initially attacked the village on August 29, but an uncharacteristically spirited Azerbaijani defense by the village self-defense force and Azerbaijani army units repulsed the Karabakh Armenians. Although many Azerbaijani soldiers were killed along with some civilians, the people in the village thought the worst was over, and decided to stay. But a second attack came on September 1.

> I was having lunch when the attack started. There was shelling and bombing. Later, at twilight, several [Karabakh] Armenian tanks and BTRs appeared outside the village and started to fire. We hid, and the minute it became dark enough we ran out of the village south down the Akera [river]. There was firing, and dead bodies along the ground. Mostly people older than myself. We walked and ran in the high grass along the river. When we got to the mill we saw the body of Javanshir Rustamov. You could see flames coming from village.[128]

Seli walked most of the next two days until she reached the relative safety of the Araks river on September 3, 1993.

MORE DISPLACED AZERIS-SEPTEMBER 1993

Azerbaijan faced another displaced person crisis that September because of Karabakh's August offensive. As in the Karabakh Armenian offensive against Kelbajar province four months earlier, topography exacerbated the suffering and complicated people's escape. Where mountains, snow, and cold presented the greatest challenge in Kelbajar, in southern Azerbaijan geography — this time the Araks river — proved the greatest obstacle to escaping civilians.

The Azeris displaced in the August 1993 offensive were trapped between the Araks river (the Iranian border) to the south, hostile Armenia to the west, and Karabakh Armenian forces advancing from the north. Only a thin finger of land stretched along the Araks river towards the east and safety, but Karabakh Armenian

---

[127]*Guardian* reporter Jonathan Rugman was in the Khanlik area during this period and filed a story titled, "Nowhere to hide for Azeri Refugees," *Guardian* (London), September 3, 1993. His reporting — based on numerous interviews with refugees — recounts a story similar to Seli's.

[128]Displaced persons camp, Saatli, Azerbaijan, March 30, 1994.

forces shelled it from time to time. [129] Artillery fire even fell on Iranian territory.

In August 1993 the ICRC reported that "some 60,000 people are fleeing eastward from Fizuli and Jebrayil to seek refuge in regions unaffected by the fighting. . . . The clashes continue to claim many civilian and military victims."[130] A western reporter at the scene described the exodus: "Since the offensive began, the narrow road has been jammed with trucks and carts piled high with livestock and furniture. In fields alongside the roadside, just twenty miles from the fighting, thousands of refugees have set up makeshift homes."[131] Mahmoud Al-Said, U.N. representative in Azerbaijan, observed, "Typically the locals would try and stay about fifteen miles from their last camp, always hoping that the next day they might return."[132]

By the end of August 1993, over 60,000 displaced persons had made their way to Imishli, an Azerbaijani town close to the Iranian border and about one hundred kilometers east of the fighting. For now, displaced persons camps have replaced the cotton that once grew in fields outside Imishli.[133] Fearful of possible social unrest from the refugees should they reach Baku that August, the Azerbaijani government set up roadblocks outside the city to prevent further passage eastward.[134] Faced with a mass of would-be refugees pressing against its northern border, which is largely populated by ethnic Azeris, Iran quickly agreed to set up camps in Azerbaijan for 100,000.[135] Turkey quickly followed suit, and the Turkish Red Crescent prepared for a humanitarian intervention.[136] Today the Turkish, Iranian, and Saudi Red Crescent societies with government support operate large displaced persons camps in

---

[129]During this first phase of the offensive, Armenian forces did not cut this route east for any length of time.

[130]ICRC Press Release, Communication to the Press No. 93/25, "Nagorny-Karabakh Conflict: 60,000 Civilians Flee Fighting in Southwestern Azerbaijan," Geneva, August 19, 1993.

[131]Simon Marks and Emma Gray, "As a Key Azeri City Falls, War Threatens to Widen," *Christian Science Monitor*, Boston, August 25, 1993, p.1.

[132]"Refugees on Move in Azerbaijani War," *The New York Times*, September 16, 1993.

[133]Sokhbet Mamedov, "V Fizuli begut ot voiny," *Izvestiya*, Moscow, August 28, 1993, p. 1.

[134]*The New York Times*, September 16, 1993, op. cit.

[135]These camps later housed civilians who arrived in Iran, fleeing the October 1993 Karabakh Armenian offensive against Zangelan province. The Iranian government quickly transported those refugees to the camps near Imishli.

[136]Ankara Turkish Radio and Television, September 17, 1993, in FBIS-SOV-93-180, September 20, 1993, p. 67.

Azerbaijan.[137]

DIPLOMATIC RESPONSES TO THE FIGHTING

In an August 18 public statement, the U.N. Security Council took the position "condemn[ing] the attack on the Fizuli region from the Nagorno-Karabakh region of the Azerbaijani Republic. . . [and] demand[ing] a stop to all attacks and an immediate cessation of the hostilities and bombardments."[138] Iran also pressured Armenia and the Karabakh Armenians to halt the offensive. Veiled threats first appeared in the English-language Tehran *Kayhan International*: "If our peace and border security is going to be threatened. . . our leaders cannot afford to let the situation take care of itself." This statement was followed by official warnings from the Iranian Foreign Ministry, accompanied by military reinforcements along Iran's borders with Azerbaijan and Armenia.[139] Turkey also reinforced its border with Armenia, and Prime Minister Ciller threatened that Turkey would not "sit with its arms crossed."[140] The U.S. State Department published a letter from Secretary of State Christopher calling on the Karabakh Armenians to adopt "a more constructive approach" to the conflict.[141]

Against the backdrop of international efforts to end the fighting, Russia pursued its own peace initiative, spearheaded by Vladimir Kazimirov, Russia's special envoy to the Karabakh conflict.[142] Increased Iranian involvement and the departure of

---

[137]The Iranian Red Crescent runs several displaced persons camps in Saatli and Imishli. The Turkish Red Crescent operates two camps outside of Barda and Agjabedi. The Saudi Red Crescent has a camp in Barda.

[138]"U.N. Demands Armenians Give up Conquests." *The New York Times*, August 19, 1993, p. 14.

[139]Lee Hockstader. "Major Offensive Laid to Armenians," *Washington Post*, August 20, 1993, p. 26; "Iran Warns Armenian Over Azerbaijan Issue," *The New York Times*, September 8, 1993; "Sosredotocheniye Voisk na irano-Azerbaidzhanskoi Granitse vyzybayet Trevogu," *Izvestiya*, Moscow, September 4, 1993, p.2.

[140]Serge Schmemann. "Turkey Holds Talks on Caucasus War," *The New York Times*, September 10, 1993.

[141]*Ibid.*

[142]Russia's increased role also reflected the change in Russian-Azeri relations resulting from the coup that ousted elected President Elchibey, considered pro-Turkish and cool at best towards Moscow. His successor Aliyev was widely viewed as pro-Moscow.
Aliyev met with President Yeltsin on September 6, 1993 and hailed a new turn in

the anti-Russian Elchibey explain this development. These Russian efforts paralleled and sometimes conflicted with the OSCE Minsk Group's work.[143] A shaky cease-fire — for which Kazimirov claimed credit — was announced on August 31, 1993, to be accompanied by a partial pullback of Karabakh Armenian forces.[144] After a September 6, 1993, meeting with President Yeltsin, Aliyev officially announced his willingness to meet with the Karabakh Armenians directly and renounced a military solution to the conflict.[145] Arkady Gukasyan, the breakaway Karabakh "Republic's" foreign minister, responded positively to Aliyev's offer.[146] On September 13, 1993, bilateral Azerbaijani-Karabakh talks — a first — were held in Moscow under the aegis of the Russian Foreign Ministry. Until then Azerbaijan refused to meet with the Karabakh Armenians, fearing to legitimize their rebellion.[147]

The Karabakh-Azerbaijan talks seemed to stabilize the situation, at least temporarily. The most important result of the negotiations was the continuation of the cease-fire until October 5, 1993.[148] Karen Baburyan, acting chairman of the Karabakh

---

relations between the two countries as he anticipated Russian participation in ending the war. He also predicted Azerbaijan's entry into the CIS, which former President Elchibey had rejected. On September 20, 1993, the Azerbaijani parliament voted thirty-one to thirteen to join the CIS, and Azerbaijan became a member.

Some have speculated that Aliyev viewed Azerbaijan's joining the CIS as *quid pro quo* payment for Russian aid in winning or ending the war. While joining the CIS was not widely unpopular in Azerbaijan, another Russian demand was: return of Russian border troops and military units to the country. Aliyev still has not assented to this request and is even leery of Russian peacekeepers in Azerbaijan, though will accept them with international observers.

See Lair Kononenko, "G. Aliyev: 'U Menya takoye Oshchushcheniye, bydto Ya i ne vykhodil iz Kremlya'" and Sokhbet Mamedov, "Klyuch k Resheniyu problem Azerbaidzhana nakhoditsya v Moskve," *Izvestiya*, Moscow, September 7, 1993, p. 2.

[143]At its September 28, 1993 meeting, the Minsk Group set forth an adjusted set of urgent measures to end the conflict and bring about a withdrawal of forces. *See* Migdalovitz, p. 6.

[144]Jonathan Rugman, "Suspicions persist as Armenians pull back," *The Guardian* ,London, September 3, 1993.

[145]John Lloyd, "Azeris offer Peace Talks," *The Financial Times*, London, September 9, 1993.

[146]Snark News Agency, Yerevan, September 4, 1993, in FBIS-SOV-93-171, September 7, 1993, p. 7.

[147]Daniel Schneider, "At Russia's Prodding, Caucasus Rivals Talk," *The Christian Science Monitor*, Boston, September 21, 1993, p. 7.

[148]*Izvestiya*, Moscow, September 15, 1993, p. 1.

parliament, commented that, "If we sit down at [the] negotiating table with the Azerbaijani side, then we hope that the situation will change for the better."[149] On October 5, both Azerbaijan and the Karabakh Armenians agreed to prolong the cease-fire another month, until November 5.[150]

KARABAKH ARMENIAN FORCES DRIVE TO THE IRANIAN BORDER AND SEIZE ZANGLEAN PROVINCE - OCTOBER 1993

The peace was short-lived. After the Karabakh Armenian's August 1993 offensive, only Zangelan province, situated in far western Azerbaijan on the Armenian border, and a thin sliver of land along the Araks river leading to Zangelan, remained unoccupied. After an ill-planned Azerbaijani offensive failed in October, Karabakh Armenian forces pushed to the Araks river and seized Zangelan and all remaining territory, setting off another wave of fleeing Azeri civilians, this time into Iran.

By the end of October, Karabakh Armenian forces had captured all the remaining Azerbaijani territory between Karabakh and the Araks rivers, the border between Azerbaijan and Iran. During this offensive, they forcibly evicted the civilian population, took hostages, killed civilians with indiscriminate fire, and looted and burned civilian property.

On October 9, just four days after the cease-fire was prolonged for a month, fighting broke out in the area, with both sides trading accusations of guilt.[151] On October 14, the U.N. Security Council issued a third resolution on the conflict, U.N. Resolution 874, based on the OSCE Minsk Group's October 1 letter. The resolution condemned the fighting, calling on both sides to accept the OSCE Minsk Group's "Adjusted Timetable of Urgent Steps." Armenia accepted the proposal, the Karabakh authorities adopted a wait-and-see approach, and Azerbaijan rejected it because the "Adjusted Timetable" linked the withdrawal of Karabakh Armenian forces from occupied Azerbaijani territory with the lifting of Azerbaijan's embargo of Armenia. The Azerbaijani government complained of being treated like "the defeated side."[152]

Serious fighting erupted again a week later. On October 21 a battalion of Afghan "mujahideen" mercenaries spearheaded a surprise attack against the Karabakh

---

[149]Itar-Tass, Moscow, September 20, 1993, in FBIS-SOV-93-181, September 21, 1993, p. 50.

[150]Itar-Tass, Moscow, October 5, 1993, in FBIS-SOV-93-192, October 6, 1993, p. 23.

[151]Snark News Agency, Yerevan, October 9, 1993, and Moscow Itar-Tass, October 11, 1993, in FBIS-SOV-93-197, p. 83 and p. 86, respectively.

[152]Sokhbet Mamedov, "Azerbaijan does not consider itself the defeated side." *Izvestiya*, Moscow, October 20, 1993, p.2, in FBIS-SOV-93-203, October 22, 1993, p. 77.

Armenian line in Jebrayil province.[153] Karabakh Armenian forces counterattacked two days later, cutting the thin strip of land along the Araks river — the escape route to the rest of Azerbaijan — and seizing Zangelan province.[154] An estimated 60,000 Azeris were forced to flee over the Araks river into Iran. By the beginning of November a considerable swath of the Iranian-Azerbaijani border up to the railway station at Horadiz was in Karabakh Armenian hands, and no Azeris save hostages were left in these provinces.

A key goal of the Karabakh Armenian offensive was the rail junction at Horadiz, the capture of which would cut off the main escape route for the inhabitants of Zangelan province and for Azeri military units.[155] The Karabakh Armenians would then control a major bridge into Iran, the capture of which would complicate Azerbaijani efforts to resupply Nakhichevan, part of Azerbaijan separated from the country by the Zangezur region of Armenia.[156]

Before the start of the Karabakh Armenian offensive on October 23, Karabakh Armenian authorities reportedly made radio broadcasts to the Azeri population ordering them to leave the area.[157] Those who heard and heeded the warning were able to escape into Iran using the Horadiz bridge. Subsequently, the bridge was destroyed by Karabakh Armenian shelling, and Azeri refugees were forced to swim across the Araks river to escape. Many drowned.

On October 23, the Karabakh Armenian offensive caught the Rustamov family on the road heading east at the Jebrayil province village of Mahmudlu, on the Iranian border about twenty-five kilometers from Horadiz station. The Rustamov family had been at a wedding party in a suburb of Zangelan on the evening of October

---

[153]Daniel Schneider, "Afghan Fighters Join Azeri-Armenian War." *The Christian Science Monitor*, Boston, November 16, 1993, p.7. See footnote, page 80.

[154]Before Armenia's October 1993 offensive, the area of southwest Azerbaijan unoccupied by Karabakh Armenian forces resembled a pot, Zangelan Province, with a handle, the unoccupied parts of Qubatli, Jebrayil, and Fizuli provinces, jutting out to the northeast along the Araks River.

[155]There are two Horadiz in the vicinity: the small village of Horadiz, about five kilometers north of the Araks River, the Iranian border, and the larger town of Horadiz, which is a rail junction and site of a major bridge into Iran. Here the latter is discussed. The railway junction was recaptured by Azeri forces during their December 1993-February 1994 offensive. The small village was not.

[156]The Azeris had been sending supplies by rail to Horadiz, then loading them on trucks for transshipment to Nakhichevan through Iran. Seizing the railway junction and bridge would end this practice and considerably lengthen the resupply route to Nakhichevan.

[157]Interview with several foreign aid workers and diplomats in Zangelan province and its vicinity during the offensive. Interviews, Azerbaijan, March 1994.

22 and were returning home to Baku on the morning of October 23 when Karabakh Armenian forces fired upon them and took them hostage:

> My brother Bakhadur Akhmedov, an officer in the Azerbaijani army, gave us a ride back to Baku. He was in uniform, but he was driving a civilian car, a Zhiguli. There was another soldier, Murshad Toptugov, my husband Kerim, and our two children, Leyla, twelve, and Kamil, eight. It was about 3:30 P.M., when we were shot at. No warning, nothing. Everyone was wounded, my daughter severely. Soldiers surrounded our car. They took Bakhadur away. We were taken to a hospital in Hadrut, where they operated on Leila. After that we were taken to Stepanakert.[158]

The family was held in Kirkizhan, near Stepanakert, at the home of Rafik Sarkissian, who wanted hostages to trade for his brother who had been captured by Azerbaijanis. On December 8, 1993, the hostage exchange was made.

Sixty-year-old Cherkez, the village elder in Buyuk Merjanli, Jebrayil Province, said that the village suffered indiscriminate attacks by Karabakh Armenian forces that killed several civilians and destroyed civilian property. Before the war, Buyuk Merjanli was home to about 7,000 Azeris; after the provincial capital Jebrayil fell at the end of August, most people fled. Only about 200 were left in the village when the Karabakh Armenians attacked.

> The front was about seven or eight kilometers from us when fighting started on October 23. Initially we heard some firing in the distance, then it became quiet. We thought our troops had advanced. But we were wrong. The [Karabakh] Armenians started to shell our village heavily, shells were landing about 200 meters from my house. Some were killed. Houses were burning. I had to crouch on the ground. Around 7:00 P.M. Azeri soldiers passed through our village, retreating. As the shelling continued we all fled for the Araks river, where we spent the night.[159]

All that night, Cherkez and the villagers of Buyuk Merjanli waited in fear by the Araks river. A couple of kilometers away they could see their homes burning. When morning broke on October 24, they could see tanks in the village. A panic erupted.

> Everybody just plunged into the water. We had no other choice.

---

[158]Interview, Baku, Azerbaijan, March 28, 1994.

[159]Interview, refugee camp, Saatli, Azerbaijan, March 29, 1993.

The bridge was already in [Karabakh] Armenian hands. We were
cut off: [Karabakh] Armenians were in Mahmudlu to the south and
Horadiz to the north. I took my clothes off and tried to walk along
the bottom, but the current was strong. I made it to the other side
and safety in Iran, but two high school boys drowned. All that day
we went to the river bank on the Iranian side to help people.
Another girl drowned crossing, plus a woman. Their bodies were
on the bank.

Iranian authorities on the Iranian side of the Araks distributed food and dry
clothes and also assisted people in crossing the river. In the first two days of the
offensive, the Tehran newspaper *Hamchari* reported that 10,000 refugees had crossed
the Araks river into Iran.[160]

Karabakh Armenian troops also seized Qazaklar, a small village of about 200
homes on the Iranian border about four kilometers south of Horadiz station, on
October 23. Elham Bairamov,[161] a soldier serving in the Azerbaijani Ministry of
Interior forces, said he was spending the last days of his twenty-day leave at home but
had to flee when the Karabakh Armenians advanced.

We were making kebab for lunch just before the attack started.
Some retreating Azerbaijani soldiers appeared and asked for some
bread, which we gave them. They told us not to drink — we had a
bottle of vodka to go along with the kebab — because we all would
have to cross the river soon. Those left in the village fled towards
the river, first the civilians, then the soldiers. People were running
and hiding, there was shooting. I swam across the river, maybe it
was 3:00 P.M. Many drowned.[162]

In the confusion, Elham lost track of his father and went back to the Qazaklar
to look for him. On the way he saw many dead Azeri civilians, including some who
appeared to have been shot at close range.

Qazaklar is only about half a kilometer from the river. I ran and hid
as I made my way back. There were many dead bodies. There was
one tractor that had been pulling a cart. It had been carrying three

---

[160]"Armenier kesseln Aserbaidschaner ein," *Sueddeutsche Zeitung*, Munich, October 27,
1993, p. 9.

[161]Pseudonym at request of witness.

[162]Interview, displaced persons camp (name withheld at request of interviewee), Azerbaijan,
April 1994.

men, three kids, and two women. When I reached them they were all dead. It seemed they had been shot by rifles at fairly close range. I found their bodies close to the river. I never found my father.[163]

The Karabakh Armenians struck Horadiz station on October 25. Shelling, which started a few days before, inflicted civilian casualties, including one witness' two sons and father. According to Tofik,

> The shelling became very heavy by October 24. Some were landing twenty-five, thirty meters from my house, which is close to the border. I went out a couple of times to find out the news and saw the bodies of those killed. The next day they entered the town with tanks. We could see some [Karabakh] Armenian soldiers about one hundred to 200 meters away. I knew my family had to leave, but there was an awful lot of firing going on outside, maybe more than the day before. We could make it to the river by running between some warehouses and some steel pipes piled high, but we had to cross an exposed area to get there. We were shot crossing the open-spot. My two sons, Vagif, four, and Vidadi, six, were killed. So was my father Meherem Farhadov. He was fifty-eight.[164]

During these advances, looting and burning continued in occupied Azeri territory. Forty-two-year-old Takhir, a plumber, remained in Soltanli village about two kilometers from the Araks river with other men after most others fled on August 23. (Often men stayed in the village to safeguard possessions.) According to Takhir, "For much of the next two months, every day I could see smoke rising from the villages north of us in Jebrayil province. Thick black smoke."[165] Those were the villages being looted and burned by Karabakh Armenian forces.[166]

---

[163] The interview was conducted in Russian, and the interviewee used the term "v upor", which translates as "at point blank range." He reported seeing cartridge shells on the ground around the vehicle.

[164] These may have been victims of crossfire but because the two children shot were so much smaller than adults, it should not have been difficult for the attackers to distinguish them from combatants. Attackers are under a duty to distinguish civilians from combatants at all times. *See* Appendix A, International Law.

[165] Interview, displaced persons camp, Saatli, Azerbaijan, March 30, 1994.

[166] Although there has been no free access to areas captured by Karabakh Armenian forces, evidence of intentional destruction was uncovered when aid agency representatives visited Horadiz Station. Horadiz Station fell to Armenian forces in October 1993 and was recaptured by Azeris in early 1994. The aid workers reported that many of the homes they saw at Horadiz

On October 25, the chairman of Nagorno-Karabakh's defense committee stated that his forces were in firm control of forty kilometers of the Iranian-Azerbaijani border.[167] Approximately 60,000 people — overwhelmingly Azeri civilians with some soldiers — were trapped in Zangelan.

On October 28, the Karabakh Armenian forces resumed their operation to seize Zangelan and force out its population.[168] The Karabakh Armenian troops came from the north, the east, and the west. Early on October 28, they hit Alibeyli, Zangelan province, a village of about 500 families about ten kilometers northeast of Zangelan just south of the Akera River. The Azerbaijani front line, where a detachment of soldiers was stationed, was located in the hills outside the village. Aydin, fifty-two, was one of the last to flee the village as Karabakh Armenians shelled it and set fire to the houses.

> It was morning, about 10:00 A.M. I had just taken my sheep out to the field. Then the shelling started. Tanks had appeared from three sides. Houses started to catch fire and burn. People fled towards the Araks [river], which is about seven kilometers away. We stayed at the border until around 4:00 P.M., then we crossed into Iran. Many drowned when we crossed. We had nothing. We had to leave everything.[169]

Refugees like Aydin who fled to Iran were quickly returned by bus to Azerbaijan, where they were settled in displaced persons camps such as Imishli.

The seizure of Zangelan ended the Karabakh Armenian campaigning season for that year.[170] They then controlled more than 20 percent of Azerbaijan.[171] By seizing

---

Station had been intentionally set on fire from the inside.

[167]RFE/RL Daily Report, Munich, October 26, 1993.

[168]"Neue armenische offensive in Aserbaidschan." *Sueddeutsche Zeitung,* Munich, November 2, 1993, p.8.

[169]Interview, refugee camp, Saatli, Azerbaijan, March 29, 1994.

[170]At the beginning of November 1993, the Azerbaijani government released casualty and refugee displaced person figures for the conflict from 1988. According to that report, 16,000 Azeris had been killed and 22,000 wounded. The report also listed 1,000,000 Azeri displaced persons and refugees in the country who had fled from Armenia, Nagorno-Karabakh, and the Azeri provinces bordering Nagorno-Karabakh.

[171]Exactly how much of the territory of Azerbaijan the Armenians hold is often debated. The Karabakh Armenians claim ten percent, since they consider Nagorno-Karabakh to be independent. The Azerbaijani government states twenty percent, which breaks down into ten

Kelbajar province, friendly Armenia now constituted Karabakh's western border. The capture of Agdam pushed Azerbaijani forces out of artillery range of Stepanakert. The push south to the Araks river eliminated Karabakh's southern front.[172]

These military operations had serious human rights consequences. As a result of 1993 Karabakh Armenian offensives — often supported by the Republic of Armenia — all the territory surrounding Karabakh on the west, east, and south was seized and over 500,000 Azeri civilians were forcibly displaced. Hundreds of Azeri civilians were taken hostage, and many were killed by indiscriminate fire. Whole cities, such as Agdam, were systematically looted and burned.

Peace efforts were again unsuccessful. After the Zangelan offensive, the OSCE Minsk Group convened and issued a new timetable of "urgent measures" to end the conflict.[173] Armenia and Karabakh accepted them. Azerbaijan rejected them.[174] On November 12, 1993, the United Nations Security Council passed Resolution 884, condemning the recent offensive and calling for the implementation of the Minsk Group's "urgent measures."[175] Little resulted from these efforts, and periodic fighting and shelling continued along the whole front.

AZERBAIJAN'S DECEMBER 1993 OFFENSIVE

A large-scale Azerbaijani offensive that commenced in late December 1993 lasted until mid-February 1994. It was fought in depopulated areas, and thus had little direct effect on civilian populations. Combat, however, was especially fierce, and many believe there were abuses and even summary execution of prisoners of war.[176]

While foreign involvement has always been a factor in the conflict in

---

percent Nagorno-Karabakh and ten percent the Azeri provinces that surround it.

[172]Nagorno-Karabakh State Defense Committee Chairman Kocharian commented, "A counterattack ended with all Azerbaijani regions to the south of Karabakh being occupied all the way to the Iranian border. . . . As a result, we sharply reduced the front line. Earlier, we had to hold the line from the Armenian border to Fizuli, 130 kilometers. Now we only have to hold the section from Fizuli to the Iranian border, only twenty-two kilometers." *Golos Armenii*, Yerevan, February 1, 1994.

[173]Migdalovitz, p. 1.

[174]*Ibid*. Azerbaijan rejected the measures because no mention was made of the former Azerbaijani community in Nagorno-Karabakh or of Karabakh Armenian withdrawal from Lachin and Shusha.

[175]United Nations Security Council Resolution 884. S/RES/884 (1993). November 12, 1993.

[176]See Chapter IV, Hostages, Prisoners of War, and Other Captives.

Nagorno-Karabakh, it reached a high point in the fighting that began in December 1993 and continued into 1994. Two groups appeared on the battlefield in significant numbers after the start of Azerbaijan's December 1993 offensive: Afghan mujahideen fighting as mercenaries for Azerbaijan;[177] and troops from the Army of the Republic of Armenia on the Karabakh side.[178]

---

[177]In situations of armed conflict (international or not). Human Rights Watch is neutral on the use by either party of mercenary soldiers. We research and report, however, on violations of the laws of war committed by mercenaries. For a greater explanation of Human Rights Watch policy on mercenaries, see Chapter VI, "Violations of the Laws of War by Foreign Actors." Human Rights Watch/Helsinki was unable to document human rights abuses by Afghans fighting as mercenaries, though we will continue to monitor their activity.

Afghan mujahideen soldiers — well-trained and acquainted with Soviet weapons — were recruited by the Azerbaijani Government and are involved in the fighting. The Afghan soldiers hired by the Azerbaijani army fit the international legal definition of mercenary because they are clearly not motivated by religious or ideological reasons. There are reports that the Afghans are appalled by the Azeris' lack of religious fervor and slack Islamic ways weakened by seventy years of Soviet secularization. The Azerbaijani government denies their participation, although informed sources believe they reportedly number from 1,500-2,500. Their headquarters was reportedly near the village of Bash-Karvend, north of Agdam, until till it fell to Karabakh forces in April 1994.

Afghan men wearing some parts of fatigues are frequently seen in Baku. During its March/April 1994 visit to Azerbaijan, on several occasions Human Rights Watch/Helsinki saw groups of young Afghan men in a mix of traditional dress and combat fatigues at the Hotel Azerbaijan in Baku. We also saw several Afghans in the courtyard of the Azerbaijani Defense Ministry and in the city of Barda.

The Afghans first arrived in Azerbaijan in the fall of 1993, after the Azerbaijani deputy foreign minister Rovshan Jivadov traveled to Afghanistan and arranged with then Prime Minister Gulbiddin Hekmatyar for Afghan fighters to come to Azerbaijan. The fighters reportedly come from the conservative Hezb-i-Wahdat faction, allied with Hekmatyar.

The Afghans spearheaded an unsuccessful offensive in October 1993; after the offensive, Karabakh Armenian forces captured documents in Pahstun and Dari, photographs of the Afghan fighters at various sites in Azerbaijan, and lists of military terms translated from Azeri into Dari.

During the Azerbaijani December 1993 offensive, mujahideen reportedly played a key role in recapturing the rail junction at Horadiz. Allegedly, the mujahideen are used to stiffen Azeri forces. In May 1994 the Karabakh forces reported capturing an Afghan mercenary.

In addition, Turkish officers and retired American officers associated with an oil company reportedly trained Azeri forces. Mercenaries from Ukraine, Russia, and Byelorussia reportedly fought on both sides.

See, Jon Auerbach, "Azerbaijan hires Afghan Mujahideen to fight Armenia," *Boston Globe,* November 8, 1993; Daniel Schneider, "Afghan Fighters Join Azeri-Armenian War, *The Christian Science Monitor,* Boston, November, 16, 1993; Moscow Interfax, FBIS-SOV-94-087, May 5, 1994, p. 49.

[178]See Chapter VII.

By mid-December 1993, fighting started again along the front, especially in the Beilagan region about forty kilometers east of Fizuli. Both sides accused each other of resuming an offensive.[179] Karabakh Armenian forces pushed closed to Beilagan, firing on the town and indiscriminately hitting the hospital. Several civilians were killed.[180]

On December 22, Azerbaijan launched a coordinated and sustained offensive along the entire length of the front.[181]

Fighting lasted until mid-February 1994, and for the first time since June 1992 Karabakh Armenian forces were forced to retreat. In the heaviest and most costly

---

[179]RFE/RL Daily Report, 12-13-93; "Na Armyano-Azerbaidzhanskom Fronte Vozobnovilis' ozhestochennye boi," *Izvestiya*, Moscow, December 14, 1993, p.1.

[180]Interview with foreign aid worker who was in Beilagan when it was shelled in December 1993. Interview, Barda, Azerbaijan, March 29, 1994.

[181]During November and December 1993, Azerbaijan instituted stopgap measures to restructure and reequip what was left of its army. After a year of unbroken defeats, Azerbaijan and President Heidar Aliyev faced further humiliation unless a viable military deterrent to Karabakh forces could be mustered. In an address before the nation, President Aliyev admitted past mistakes and promised tough new measures, including the sacking of a number of high-level officers and the empowering of state security organs to punish treachery and instill discipline in military ranks.

> It must be noted that our defeats are due, on the one hand, to weakness and the Azerbaijani Army units' lack of fighting and skill...It is no secret that our soldiers and fighters in Jebrayil Raion and in Horadiz and elsewhere abandoned the civilians and fled the battle zones without putting up any fight....It would have been possible to create an army over two or three years (from the beginning of the conflict in 1988) and defend Azerbaijan. But this opportunity was lost, and Azerbaijan's defense has suffered rather than improved. Various groups and battalions fought independently of each other. They served various forces and goals and lacked an overall military strategy.

Work was continued on disarming unauthorized military units or putting them under the authority of the Azerbaijani ministry of defense. Restrictions were placed on restaurants, bars, and other places of entertainment in Baku. A defense council was formed.

On December 6, 1993, the Azerbaijani National Assembly instituted military censorship. Mobilization was announced, and restrictions imposed on those under forty leaving the country. Press gang raids were a common occurrence, with young men being pulled off buses and stopped in public places for induction. New arms were purchased to replace those lost to the enemy.

See also, "Aliyev kritikuyet Azerbaidzhanskuyu Armiyu," *Izvestiya*, Moscow, November 11, 1993, p. 1.

fighting of the seven-year conflict,[182] Azerbaijani forces managed initial impressive gains, capturing the vital rail junction at Horadiz and strategic heights around Agdam and Mardakert. They even managed to push south of the Murov mountains into Kelbajar province, seizing the all-important Omar pass.

As a result, calls went out in Karabakh, the Republic of Armenia, and the Armenian diaspora for volunteers, and the maximum age of conscription in Karabakh was increased from forty-three to fifty.[183] During a February 1994 trip to London, Armenian President Ter-Petrosyan stated that Armenia would intervene militarily if the Karabakh Armenians were faced with "forced deportation" or "genocide."[184] According to our research, regular Armenian army forces were deployed in the fighting.[185]

---

[182]While no exact casualty figures exist, most estimates by aid workers, foreign embassies, and journalists put the number of dead for this offensive at roughly 600-800 for Karabakh Armenian forces and possibly 4,000-6,000 for the Azeris. The commonly used formula of three wounded to one dead would result in 1,800-2,400 injured Armenians and 12,000-18,000 injured Azeris.

[183]*Yerkir*, Yerevan, Armenia, January 1, 1994, in Armenian Assembly of American Daily News Summary, January 14, 1994.

[184]AZG, February 11,1994, in "Daily News Report from Armenia: Armenian Assembly of America," February 11, 1994.

[185]See Chapter VII, The Republic of Armenia as a Party to the Conflict.

III. DEVELOPMENTS IN 1994

By mid-February, Karabakh forces — with the aid of troops from the Republic of Armenia — had pushed back most of Azerbaijan's advances from its December 1993 offensive. Of all its major gains, the Azeris managed only to hold the railhead at Horadiz. A Russian -brokered cease-fire on February 16, 1994 stopped major fighting, but some skirmishing continued.

In mid-April 1994, heavy fighting broke out near Agdam and Mardakert, which turned into an Karabakh Armenian offensive by the beginning of May. Karabakh Armenian forces — again with the support of forces from the Republic of Armenia — pushed north about two-thirds up the Agdam-Barda road and recaptured several villages in Mardakert area of Nagorno-Karabakh. Karabakh Armenian forces also pushed into Terter and Geranboi (Shaumyan) provinces, Azerbaijan.[186]

This fighting resulted in another 50,000 Azeri displaced persons, some of whom had fled earlier offensives. The ICRC representative in the area commented, "We were just beginning to deal with the 100,000 or so who came last year. We have distributed 3,200 tents but it is not enough."[187]

Jane Olson, Human Rights Watch/Helsinki Board member, travelled to Azerbaijan in June 1994 for the Women's Commission for Refugee Women and Children and spoke with the Azeri displaced from the April-May 1994 offensive. The displaced reported attacks against civilians by indiscriminate fire and hostage-taking.[188] The still-burning villages of the displaced were visible from where Ms. Olson conducted her interview.

Since early-May 1994 the guns in Karabakh have largely been silent with the exception of some minor skirmishing and flare-ups. Russian Defense Minister Pavel Grachev worked out a cease-fire on May 16, 1994. On July 27, 1994, the defense ministers of Armenia and Azerbaijan and the head of Karabakh's armed forces signed another cease-fire agreement giving legal status to the accord worked out in

---

[186]Many analysts believed that the offensive was a Karabakh Armenian attempt to seize the city of Yevlakh, effectively cutting Azerbaijan in two and separating the capital Baku from Azerbaijan's second city, Ganje. Neither goal was achieved.

In a thought-provoking op-ed, Moorad Mooradian argues that Russia wanted Karabakh forces to take Yevlakh, but Armenian President Ter-Petrosyan and Robert Kocharian, head of Karabakh's defense committee, refused. See, "Rumors?", *The Armenian Mirror-Spectator*, September 17, 1994.

[187]Lawrence Sheets, "Thousands of Azeri Refugees Trapped in Karabakh War," Reuters, April 30, 1994.

[188]Interview with Jane Olson. *See also* "Families at Risk: Fleeing the Nagorno-Karabakh Conflict," Women's Commission for Refugee Women and Children, June 1994.

May; in August 1994, representatives from Armenia, Azerbaijan, and Nagorno-Karabakh met in Moscow under the mediation of the Russian Federation to work on the draft of a "Major Political Agreement" to end the war.[189] On September 8, 1994, Presidents Ter-Petrosyan and Aliyev of Armenia and Azerbaijan met for closed-door talks in Moscow to resolve the Karabakh conflict; reportedly, the two still had major differences, especially concerning the status of Lachin and Shusha and the composition of a future peacekeeping force.[190] The Azerbaijani side demanded the return of the strategically-important towns of Lachin and Susha, but the Karabakh Armenians objected to this. In December 1994, the OSCE decided to dispatch a 3,000-strong multinational peacekeeping force.[191]

---

[189]RFE/RL Daily Report, July 29, 1994; Covcas Bulletin. Geneva. August 24, 1994.

[190]"Armenia, Azerbaijan still at odds over Karabakh." Reuters, September 10, 1994.

[191]See Chapter X.

IV. HOSTAGES, PRISONERS OF WAR, AND OTHER CAPTIVES

Hostage-taking or holding is explicitly forbidden in armed conflicts.[192] Both Azerbaijan and the Karabakh rebels have violated this prohibition during the conflict. In addition, hostages have been held in the Republic of Armenia, and there are reports that Armenian forces took hostages.

A simple formula usually dictates hostage-taking: whichever side is advancing will take hostage the enemy's civilian population that is too sick, too old, or unwilling or unable to escape. While hostage-taking was about equal on both sides in 1992, in 1993 and 1994 Karabakh Armenians seized the overwhelming number of hostages due to the simple fact that they advanced into civilian areas populated by Azeris.[193]

Taking or holding hostages in an international armed conflict is also forbidden and constitutes a grave breach of the Geneva Conventions.[194] The governments of both Armenia and Azerbaijan have committed or have allowed the taking and holding of hostages, grave breaches of the Geneva Conventions.

> "Hostages" has a particular definition:
> [H]ostages are persons who find themselves, willingly or unwillingly, in the power of the enemy and who answer with their freedom or their life for compliance with the orders of the latter and for upholding the security of its armed forces.[195]

---

[192]This prohibition applies to international as well as non-international conflicts.

[193]A number of individuals of Armenian descent were taken hostage in 1993, many of them kidnapped from trains traveling through southern Russia and Georgia. According to the Armenian Republic's Karabakh committee, thirty-two ethnic Armenians were kidnapped in 1993: five from Russia; five from Armenia; twenty-two from Georgia.

Most representatives of Western embassies and humanitarian organizations with whom Human Rights Watch/Helsinki spoke believe criminal elements — not the Government of Azerbaijan — are behind such abductions. Also families on both sides who have lost relatives in the fighting might seize a hostage for barter.

[194]IV Geneva, art. 147. See Appendix A, International Law. This prohibition applies to the taking of "protected persons" as hostages, that is, those non-combatants who find themselves in the hands of a party to the conflict or occupying power of which they are not nationals. IV Geneva, art. 4 This means citizens of the Republic of Armenians in Azeri custody and Azeri citizens in Republic of Armenian custody.

[195]ICRC Commentary on the Additional Protocols, p. 874.

Persons captured and held for exchange purposes are hostages, since they answer with their freedom for compliance by others with the orders of their captors. In this conflict, captured persons are frequently held for exchange purposes. They may be exchanged for those captured by the enemy or even for the bodies of dead combatants.

We consider that those held by private parties to force others to release a relative (or body of a relative) are hostages, where the local authorities (government or rebel) are aware of the location of the captivity and the identity of the captors. Because of the power of these local authorities to terminate the private captivity, these captives are "in the power of the enemy."

Prisoners of war, that is, captured combatants treated as prisoners of war under the Third Geneva Convention, are not considered to be hostages when they are exchanged for other prisoners of war.

Prisoners of war are sometimes taken. Their treatment while in confinement is strictly regulated by the Third Geneva Convention, which categorically forbids the killing, torture, or inhumane treatment of prisoners of war.[196] During the intense fighting of Azerbaijan's two-month offensive that began in December 1993, however, almost all outside observers were troubled by the low number of captured combatants taken by both sides relative to the level and scale of combat.

Human Rights Watch/Helsinki spoke with captured combatants on both sides who were slashed with bayonets or knifes at the time of their capture. Most were beaten thereafter, sometimes to the point of unconsciousness. One released Karabakh Armenian captive reported that hot water had been poured on him while in detention. A released Azeri captive told Human Rights Watch/Helsinki that he and two of his comrades were beaten terribly, then tied to the outside of an armored personnel carrier and a tank and driven off. Prisoners were sometimes subject to ridicule and scorn from civilian crowds.

OFFICIAL HOSTAGE AND PRISONER OF WAR COMMITTEES

Until 1993, the taking, holding, and exchanging of hostages and prisoners of war was rather informal. A militiaman would capture a person, then exchange him a few days later for the body of a fallen or captured comrade. Sometimes a captured person would be "acquired" by a family that wanted a hostage to compel the return of the captured relative. Middlemen or the families themselves would work out deals and exchanges.

In 1993, however, both Azerbaijan and Nagorno-Karabakh authorities formed committees to deal with prisoners of war and hostages. While private trading

---

[196]III Geneva, articles 129-130.

still occurs, most observers believe these official committees handle the majority of prisoner of war and hostage exchanges. Both sides are quite open about hostage-taking, and excuse it because the other side does it.

The Armenian government has participated in the holding of hostages; several Azeri hostages told Human Rights Watch/Helsinki they were held in jails or other locations inside Armenia. In addition, several former Azeri hostages alleged that soldiers from the Republic of Armenia army took them hostage.

In January 1993, the Azerbaijani government formed the State Committee for Prisoners of War and Hostages under the chairmanship of the Assistant Minister for State Security Namik Abbassov.[197] In April 1993, Karabakh authorities set up a Committee for Hostages and Prisoners of War under Aleksandr Agasaryan.[198]

The main Azerbaijani prison camp for combatants and civilians captured in connection with the Karabakh conflict is located at Gobustan, an hour south of Baku. Most Azeri captured combatants are held in the Shusha prison in Nagorno-Karabakh or, if wounded, at the Stepanakert Children's Hospital; civilian hostages are kept at the main kindergarten in central Stepanakert.[199] Some prisoners of war as well as hostages have been held in Armenia.

Mr. Agasaryan and Mr. Abbassov stated that the ICRC — which has delegates in Stepanakert, Nagorno-Karabakh, in Baku and Barda, Azerbaijan, and in Yerevan, Armenia — had access to prisoners under their charge. Though the ICRC in no way takes part in hostage or prisoner trading, it does facilitate the actual physical exchange when requested by both sides.

Both sides reported limiting the private hostage-holding by families. According to the chairmen of both committees, no prisoners of war or hostages currently are exchanged without their knowledge, and they have custody of the overwhelming majority of these persons. All captured persons, both combatants and civilian hostages, are supposed to be turned over to them.

This system is not perfect, however, and on both sides private hostage-taking continues, though to a far lesser extent. Exchanges are sometimes made at the

---

[197]Interview with Namik Abbassov, Baku, Azerbaijan, March 25, 1994. Most of the following information concerning prisoners and hostages in Azerbaijani custody or Azerbaijani assertions concerning Azeri prisoners and hostages in Armenian custody comes from this interview.

[198]Interview with Mr. Agasaryan, Stepanakert, April 14, 1994. The following information concerning Azeri hostages and prisoners in Armenian custody in Nagorno-Karabakh or Armenian assertions about Armenian prisoner and hostages in Azeri custody refers to this interview unless otherwise stated.

[199]Human Rights Watch/Helsinki visited all of the above places. We did not visit Bailovskaya Prison in Baku, where several ethnic Armenians are held on charges of murder for allegedly killing a journalist and a Russian officer. They are not considered hostages, and thus are not in the custody of Abbassov's committee.

battlefield level that are never centrally reported or controlled. For example, an Azerbaijani prisoner of war who was captured on August 6, 1993 and exchanged on February 22, 1994 told Human Rights Watch/Helsinki that he was held with about ten other captured Azerbaijani combatants by a Karabakhi regiment based near a tourist resort outside of Shusha in Karabakh. He reported that he and the other men never received ICRC visits during the time he was held there.

Both sides distrust each other and dispute the number of prisoners and hostages the other still holds.[200] The Azeris claim 2,500 hostages are held in Armenia and Nagorno-Karabakh out of a total of 3,687 hostages, prisoners of war, and missing known to the Azerbaijani committee. The Karabakh Armenian side denies the existence of such a large number of hostages or prisoners in Nagorno-Karabakh or Armenia and maintains that as of April 1994 there are only around 200-225 prisoners and hostages in the custody of the Karabakh Committee on Prisoners and Hostages, all visited by the ICRC.

The Karabakh Armenians believe that Azerbaijan holds about 500 Armenians, most of them taken in 1992 or before.[201] Agasaryan, chairman of the Karabakh committee, argued, "I want to tell you why from our point of view we simply don't release the people we captured in areas of military action. Of course one could just release them all, but there are 500 of ours over there. Civilians that were taken in Mardakert province. No information about them. But when Azeri soldiers took these areas, these people were there. . ." In 1992, Human Rights Watch/Helsinki received information that fifty ethnic Armenians from Maraga, Mardakert province, were captured by Azerbaijani forces in an attack on April 10, 1992. According to the Agasaryan, many of these people are still missing.

The Azerbaijani State Committee in turn claimed (as of April 1994) to have fourteen Armenian POWs, four civilian looters captured in the battle zone on Azerbaijani territory, and possibly five other ethnic Armenians captured in Azerbaijan

---

[200]They roughly agree on those released so far. According to Agasaryan, his Karabakh commission has exchanged or released 230 individuals since the time of its formation in April 1993. Abbassov's figures roughly correspond: he stated that he received or exchanged 224 hostages and prisoners of war from both Karabakh and Armenia in 1993.

[201] Azerbaijan launched a major offensive in June 1992 that captured most of Mardakert province, the northern most region of Karabakh, and nearby Geranboi (Shaumyan) province of Azerbaijan. An estimated 40,000 Armenians were made homeless.

Human Rights Watch/Helsinki examined the Armenian-prepared list of approximately 500 Armenian prisoners and hostages allegedly held in Azerbaijan. The majority of cases were from 1992 or before, though there were cases of Armenians pulled from trains in 1993 and some instances of prisoners of war taken in 1993 and 1994.

and held until it can be determined that they are not part of a terrorist group.[202] Some of the civilian looters captured are legally Azerbaijani citizens — i.e. residents of Nagorno-Karabakh — but are not charged under Azerbaijani criminal law. Rather, they are held until they can be exchanged. Namik Abbassov, the head of the Azerbaijani committee, stated that possibly six or seven other Karabakh Armenians were held privately by families and possibly another seven or eight captured combatants were in the custody of the Azerbaijani army during their interrogation, but would ultimately come under his jurisdiction.

The Azeris feel pressure to negotiate a high number of Azeri hostages and prisoners to be exchanged for each Karabakh Armenian hostage because of the disproportion in the numbers held by each side: According to the Azeris, they hold twenty-nine Karabakh Armenians, and the Karabakh Armenians admit to having 225 Azeris.

But both sides accuse the other of holding several times that number of hostages and prisoners of war. The Azeris' reason that if hostages and prisoners were exchanged on a one-for-one basis, they would quickly run out of Karabakh Armenian captives while hundreds of Azeris would remain in Karabakh Armenian hands. Namik Abbassov stated,

> We know the names of 852 Azeris held there. What would happen if we freed their fourteen for fourteen of ours — how about the rest? . . . I therefore set the following system: We will return a single POW for one of our own POWs . . . and then we might demand five to twenty hostages . . . There aren't any laws or written rules. It's all created as we go along. . . . The Karabakh Armenians make their gradations and so do we. It might be wild for you, for the civilized West, but it's our reality.

Mr. Agasaryan countered that:

> They often set conditions which are impossible to fulfill. Basically this concerns the quantity of the exchange. For one Armenian they demand ten to fifteen Azerbaijanis. . . . They have to become convinced of the fact that we don't have such a quantity of people and that it simply can't be. It's simply because they don't want their

---

[202]Azeri fears of terrorism are not unfounded. On July 3, 1994, seven were killed and thirty wounded when a bomb exploded in a Baku metro station. Twelve were killed in a similar bombing in March 1994 in Baku.

Armenia has also suffered terror attacks. On September 4, 1994, fourteen individuals were killed when a bomb exploded in a market in the northern Armenian town of Bagrateshen.

people to know the true picture of what's happening.[203]

There has been movement, however, in the exchange and release of hostages. On August 13, 1994, in connection with the overall ceasefire talks, both sides reached an agreement to exchange or release within one week all women and children hostages.[204] On September 7, 1994, the ICRC facilitated the exchange of three Azeris (two old men and a women) and three Karabakh Armenians (two women and a girl); on September 15, 1994, Karabakh authorities released through the ICRC twenty-four Azeri female hostages, the youngest of which was 18 months old, the oldest 78 years.[205]

HOSTAGES HELD IN ARMENIA

Three elderly men interviewed by Human Rights Watch/Helsinki reported being held hostage during part of their captivity in Armenia before being exchanged. In addition, they stated that several other hostages were also held with them in Armenia. The following men spent some of their detention in Armenia: Aleksandr, an eighty-two-year-old Azerbaijani citizen of Russian descent taken hostage in Agdam, Azerbaijan, on July 23, 1993 and released in February 1994; Mr. G., who was captured in the village of Hoje, Azerbaijan, on August 30 and exchanged on October 18, 1993 (he wishes not to have his name used); Fakrat, 61, captured near Qarakishiler, Qubatli province, Azerbaijan on August 28 and exchanged on November 15, 1993.

PRISONERS OF WAR HELD IN ARMENIA

As of April 1994, there were about thirty Azeri prisoners of war in Armenia whom the ICRC regularly visits.[206] In an August 1994 meeting with Human Rights Watch General Counsel Juan Mendez, Armenian Foreign Minister Papazyan stated that Armenians held between 18-22 prisoners. Allegedly, they were captured in border skirmishes. The majority are held in the capital, Yerevan, and a few in Spitak,

---

[203]Interview, Stepanakert, Nagorno-Karabakh, April 14, 1994.

[204]COVCAS Bulletin, Geneva, August 24, 1994, p. 1.

[205]ICRC, Communication to the Press No. 94/35, September 16, 1994, Geneva, Switzerland.

[206]According to Western diplomats, there are probably some prisoners and hostages held secretly by families in Armenia.

Armenia. Until January 1994, all were in the custody of the Armenian Ministry of Defense.

On January 29, 1994, eight Azerbaijani prisoners of war died under suspicious circumstances during an alleged escape attempt in a prison camp under the jurisdiction of the Defense Ministry in Yerevan, Armenia; consequently the remaining prisoners were transferred to the custody of the Armenian Ministry of the Interior.

The killing of prisoners of war is a grave breach of the Geneva Conventions.[207] According to Armenian authorities, the eight men killed a guard, took his gun, and attempted to escape, but were immediately discovered. The Armenian military procurator alleges that seven of the men then committed serial suicide with one guard's gun after their escape attempt was foiled. Human Rights Watch/Helsinki considers this serial suicide inherently improbable.

Dr. Derrick Pounder, a Scottish forensic expert retained by the Azerbaijani government who performed autopsies in April 1994 on the eight bodies shortly after they were returned to the government of Azerbaijan, stated that the nature of wounds on six of them indicates summary execution.[208] As of this writing the Armenian government still has not issued comprehensive findings of a commission investigating the deaths.

Human Rights Watch/Helsinki considers that the deaths of the eight prisoners while in Armenian custody are the responsibility of the government of Armenia, and that if an independent commission finds malfeasance in the deaths of the eight prisoners, the government of Armenia is guilty of a grave breach of the Geneva Conventions.

Eight other Azeri prisoners have been tried and sentenced for the killing of several Armenian villagers; three received the death sentence, which has not yet been carried out. Reportedly, these eight are to be exchanged for Armenian prisoners and hostages held in Azerbaijan.

---

[207] III Geneva, article 129 and 130. Human Rights Watch/Helsinki has sent several letters to the Armenian Government presenting our findings and calling for an independent investigation. Those letters are reprinted in Appendix C.

[208] He could not absolutely exclude suicide as a cause of death, but serial suicides are extremely rare.

One of the prisoners did commit suicide, but by slitting his throat with a knife.

V. DISPLACED PERSONS AND REFUGEES[209]

The conflict over Nagorno-Karabakh has created during the past seven years an unregulated, chaotic, and often bloody exchange of populations among Armenia, Azerbaijan, and Nagorno-Karabakh. The rules of war, however, forbid the forced transfer or displacement of civilians. There are only two exceptions to the prohibition on displacement of civilians, both for tightly-regulated, war-related reasons: their security or imperative military reasons. None of the displacement meets these rigid criteria.

At this point, violent forced displacement is a *fait accompli*. An estimated 350,000 Armenians fled Azerbaijan after violent anti-Armenian pogroms in 1988 and 1990. Between 1988 and 1994 an estimated 750,000-800,000 Azeris were forced out of Nagorno-Karabakh, Armenia,[210] and seven other Azeri provinces now completely occupied by Karabakh Armenians. The pre-war population of these seven provinces was overwhelmingly Azeri.

Most of the 750,000-800,000 Azeri were displaced or made refugees as a result of violations of the rules of war by the Karabakh Armenians. All 40,000 Azeris who lived in Nagorno-Karabakh were forced out by mid-1992. A Karabakh Armenian military offensive in May/June 1992 captured a large part of Lachin province, Azerbaijan, and created another 30,000 Azeri displaced, many of Kurdish descent.

The biggest wave of displaced persons came in 1993, as Karabakh Armenian troops — often with the support of forces from the Republic of Armenia — captured the remaining Azerbaijani provinces surrounding Karabakh and forced out the Azeri civilian population: the rest of Lachin province, and Kelbajar, Agdam, Fizuli, Jebrayil, Qubatli, and Zangelan provinces. According to Azerbaijani government figures, these Karabakh Armenian offensives forced an estimated 450,000-500,000 Azeris out of their homes.[211]

---

[209]A displaced person is one who flees his home because of fear of persecution but does not cross an international border. A refugee is one who is forced out of his home under the same circumstances but crosses an international border. Thus an Armenian who fled his Baku home for Yerevan is a refugee; an Azeri who was forced out of Fizuli, Azerbaijan, and went to Baku is a displaced person.

[210] By the end of 1989, an estimated 167,000 Azerbaijanis who lived in Armenia fled the country, often under violent circumstances. Their displacement, while violent, was not a direct result of violations of the rules of war by Karabakh Armenian forces.

[211]"Information Bulletin on the Consequences of the Aggression by the Republic of Armenia Against the Azerbaijani Republic," Ministry of Foreign Affairs of the Azerbaijani Republic, Baku, Azerbaijan, February 1994.

According to the ICRC, a late April 1994 Karabakh Armenian offensive along the Agdam-Barda road and in Terter and Geranboi provinces of Azerbaijan created another 50,000 Azeri displaced.[212]

Much of the forced displacement of ethnic Armenians took place before Azerbaijan became an independent country recognized by the international community. The estimated 350,000 ethnic Armenians who lived in Azerbaijan left in two waves in 1988 and in 1990 after anti-Armenian violence.[213] Some went to Armenia, some to major Russian cities, others to southern Russia. In 1991, in Operation Ring, the government of the former Azerbaijani Soviet Socialist Republic with the aid of central authorities in Moscow was responsible for the forced displacement of Armenian civilians from Geranboi (Shaumyan) province and from Chaikent (Getashen),[214] a village in Khanlar province, Azerbaijan. Some of these individuals returned in late 1991 and early 1992. In June 1992, an Azerbaijani counteroffensive against Geranboi (Shaumyan) province and Mardakert province, Nagorno-Karabakh, displaced roughly 40,000 people. Most of these Armenians — with the exception of those in Geranboi (Shaumyan) province and Chaikent (Getashen), Khanlar province — have now returned to their villages as a result of later successful Karabakh Armenian offensives.

Article 17 of Protocol II, applicable in the internal conflict between Azerbaijan and the Karabakh rebels,[215] states:

1. The displacement of the civilian population shall not be ordered for reasons related to the conflict unless the security of the civilians involved or imperative military reasons so demand.

"Imperative military reasons" require "the most meticulous assessment of the circumstances"[216] because such reasons are so capable of abuse. One authority has

---

[212]"ICRC Concerned about Refugee Flows from Karabakh War." Reuters. May 3. 1994; "Refugees Swell on Eve of Talks," *AIS News Watch*, May 4. 1994. p. 5.

[213]According to Vladimir Movsessian, head of Main Directorate of the Armenian Republic for Refugee Questions. refugees in Armenia include 260,000 ethnic Armenian refugees from Azerbaijan, excluding areas north of Nagorno-Karabakh. 19,800 from Geranboi (Shaumyan) province. Azerbaijan. 5,000 from the village of Chaikent (Getashen) in Khanlar Province. Azerbaijan, and 16,000 from Karabakh. In April 1994, he stated that 22,000 refugees returned to their homes in Karabakh since February 1993. Interview. Yerevan. April 8. 1994.

[214]Chaikent is the official Azeri name. Getashen the unofficial Armenian one.

[215]*See* Appendix A, International Law.

[216]*ICRC Commentary*. p. 1472.

stated:

> Clearly, imperative military reasons cannot be justified by political
> motives. For example, it would be prohibited to move a population
> in order to exercise more effective control over a dissident ethnic
> group.[217]

Mass relocation or capture of civilians for the purpose of changing the ethnic composition of territory, in order to later justify annexation, is a political, not a military reason. The destruction of civilian homes for the purpose of forcing those civilians to move is as illegal as a direct order to move, and does not qualify as an "imperative military reason."

Article 17 of Protocol II also requires that,

> "Should such displacements have to be carried out, all possible
> measures shall be taken in order that the civilian population may be
> received under satisfactory conditions of shelter, hygiene, health,
> safety and nutrition."

Neither side has paid any attention whatsoever to this requirement.

In international armed conflicts, individual or mass forcible transfers and deportations of inhabitants of occupied territory to another country are prohibited. Such persons may be evacuated if their security or imperative military reasons so demand, but proper accommodations must be provided.[218]   Neither party to the international conflict has ever provided such accommodations.

Because the vast majority of displaced in 1993 were produced by Karabakh Armenian military actions, we examine their justifications, although the same rules apply equally to Azerbaijan.

Murad Petrosian, deputy commander of the Karabakh army, stated that his army did not have the forces to garrison an occupied territory with a hostile civilian population, nor the technologically-advanced weapons necessary to silence enemy fire bases without seizing the territory where they are based.[219] The availability of garrison forces and of high technology weapons in this case does not constitute "imperative" military reason. The lack of sophisticated weapons to silence enemy fire bases is militarily unrelated to the permanent displacement of the civilian population from the area of the fire base. Artillery is routinely destroyed or captured and territory seized in armed conflicts without permanent eviction of the civilian population from the area.

---

[217]*ICRC Commentary*, p. 1472.

[218]IV Geneva, art. 49.

[219]Interview, Stepanakert, April 15, 1994.

Karabakh Armenians attempt to justify this violent forced displacement by the need to hold territory for defensive military reasons and by the unavailability of adequate troops to control the presumably hostile Azeri civilian population in that territory.

Troop unavailability, however, represents a dilemma of the occupying army's own making because it is a function of the extent of military activities. In 1993, Karabakh Armenians — sometimes with the support of forces from the Republic of Armenia — were constantly on the offensive outside the boundaries of NKAO in Azerbaijani territory, an area overwhelmingly populated by Azeris. To excuse violent forced displacement of Azeris from their homes so that Karabakh Armenian troops would be freed up to take more Azeri territory mocks the protection afforded civilians by the rules of war.

The burden of providing for this staggering Azeri displaced population has fallen on the Azerbaijani government and the international community. Irshad Aliyev, chairman of the Azerbaijani State Committee for Work with Refugees and the Forcibly Displaced, told Human Rights Watch/Helsinki that his committee was completely overwhelmed by the 1993 flood of refugees. "At first families took their relatives in, then schools, hotels, pioneer summer camps, resorts, everything started to fill up with refugees. After the offensives of 1993, the Iranians, Turks, and Saudis had to help us build tent cities in Imishli, Saatli, Barda, and Agjabedi. Even then there are people living along the side of road, in little dugouts and shanties."[220] Aliyev complained that since January 1994 the state simply did not have the money to pay each refugee family registered with the government its monthly payment of 900 manat.[221] Refugees and displaced received no food parcels from the government, but the ICRC would often disburse supplemental food parcels to those living in displaced persons' camps.[222] Haji Rajabov, Head of the Azerbaijani Council of Ministers' Department for Displaced Persons and Refugees, told Human Rights Watch/Helsinki that, "We try our best. Last year we disbursed twenty billion manat. But there simply isn't any money any more."[223]

---

[220]Interview with Irshad Aliyev, chairman of Azerbaijan State Committee for work with Refugees and Forcibly Displaced, Baku, Azerbaijan, March 24, 1994. According to a UNHCR representative in Baku, based on Azerbaijan Government figures there were an estimated 658,000 Azeri displaced persons and 235,000 Azeri refugees in Azerbaijan in March 1994.

[221]The manat is Azerbaijan's inflation-plagued currency. In March 1994 one dollar bought about 500 manat, and inflation had reached triple digits.

[222]An ICRC supplemental food package is meant to augment the diet of a family of four for a month and includes such staples as lentils, cooking oil, and macaroni. In 1993 the ICRC provided assistance to approximately 170,000 persons in and around the conflict areas. 1993 ICRC Annual Report (Geneva: ICRC, 1994), p. 169.

[223]Interview, Baku, March 25, 1994.

According to Mr. Rajabov, only five to ten percent of refugees and displaced are employed.

Foreign assistance has played some role in alleviating the crisis. Iran, Turkey, and Saudi Arabia all set up displaced persons camps throughout Azerbaijan. The UNHCR, the ICRC and the European Union have offices in both Armenia and Azerbaijan. There are also several private aid groups. In addition, foreign embassies have disbursed funds for humanitarian aid to the displaced and to refugees. In May 1994 the United Nations cited Armenia and Azerbaijan among five former Soviet republics in dire need of humanitarian aid.[224]

---

[224]Philip Pullella, "U.N. Warns of Food Crisis in Ex-Soviet Republics," Reuters, May 4, 1994.

VI.   VIOLATIONS OF THE LAWS OF WAR BY FOREIGN ACTORS

In situations of armed conflict, whether international or not in nature, Human Rights Watch does not take a position on the legality or advisability of the use of mercenaries. As explained below, international humanitarian law strives to limit the use of mercenaries by denying them the "combatant's privilege;" it does not, however, prohibit them. There have been attempts to regulate or prohibit their use through international instruments but, at this stage, there are no principles of general applicability on the subject. In any event, an international standard on the use of mercenaries would address a political concern on the international community and not a human rights matter. We believe, therefore, that the issue of the use of mercenaries is outside our mandate as a human rights organization.

We do, however, research and report on violations of the laws of war committed by mercenaries, a topic within our mandate. We also call on the party that exercises command authority over mercenaries who commit abuses to punish them.

In the stage of the conflict covered by this report, Human Rights Watch/Helsinki has documented violations of the rules of war committed by Slavic combat pilots (Russians, Belorussians, or Ukrainians) hired by Azerbaijan as mercenaries. Such pilots have killed civilians with indiscriminate fire. Both sides, however, have used mercenaries,[225] and we will continue to monitor their actions for

---

[225]There has been extensive, though limited involvement of others throughout the conflict. Russian, Ukrainian, and Belorussian mercenaries or rogue units of the Soviet/Russian Army have fought on both sides.

The February 1992 massacre at Khojali, an Azeri-populated town outside of Stepanakert, in which hundreds of Azeri civilians were killed was carried out by Karabakh Armenian forces, reportedly with the support of elements of the now-disbanded 366th Motor Rifle Regiment of the Russian Army.

On September, 11, 1992, Azerbaijani forces captured six Russian special forces *(spetznaz)* troops of the 7th Russian Army based in Armenia near the village of Merjimek. The men reportedly received 75,000 Russian rubles from the Armenian Ministry of Defense for action near in the village of Srkhavend, Nagorno-Karabakh, in June 1992.

Azerbaijan also alleged involvement of Russian Army units based in Armenia during the April 1993 Karabakh Armenian seizure of Kelbajar province. As Karabakh forces became more organized, the role of outside mercenaries seems to have decreased, but they still play a role. Soldiers of Armenian descent serving in the Russian 127th Division based in Armenia were captured in Kelbajar province, Azerbaijan, in January 1994.

In late 1993, there were reports that Azerbaijan — with the help of Russian military commissariats — was recruiting mercenaries from the central Russian provinces of Ivanovo and Vladimir. *The Boston Globe* reported that Russian military trainers were training Azerbaijani troops near the city of Ganje in northern Azerbaijan, although who sent them was unclear. Both Armenian and Western sources allege that trained Slavic mercenaries operated heavy and

possible human rights violations.

Most informed observers believe that mercenaries pilot most of Azerbaijan's air force. The majority of pilots in the Azerbaijani air force are reported to be from outside Azerbaijan, serving on a contract basis. In February 1994, for example, the Armenian Defense Ministry reported shooting down an Azerbaijani Air Force SU-24 that strayed over the border near Vardenis and capturing a Tatar mercenary from Kyrgyzstan, Marat Ishkinovich.[226] On May 23, 1994, the Military Tribunal of Nagorno-Karabakh sentenced to death Yuri Belichenko, a ethnic Ukrainian who flew

---

mechanized weapons in Azerbaijan's December 1993 offensive.

Human Rights Watch/Helsinki spoke with three prisoners of war — two ethnic Russians and one Ukrainian — whom Karabakh authorities charge with being mercenaries. The interviews were conducted at Shusha Prison, Shusha, Nagorno-Karabakh, and the second floor of the Stepanakert Children's Hospital on April 15, 1994. The Ukrainian, eighteen, admitted he served in the Azerbaijani army after he fled Kiev to avoid the police. He went to Azerbaijan because he had heard that foreigners who served in its army were paid well. He had never served in the Soviet army. The two Russians denied being mercenaries, but gave rather convoluted and unlikely stories of how they ended up in the Azerbaijani army.

In 1993 there were also numerous press reports of American and British mercenaries training Azerbaijani troops. Allegedly, the American petroleum company "Megaoil," which reportedly has links with retired U.S. Army General Richard Secord, had hired retired American military personnel and was training Azerbaijani troops. The United States Justice Department is investigating the matter as a possible violation of U.S. law. *The Independent* in London in January 1994 reported a purported deal to trade British military trainers and weapons for Azerbaijani oil. Retired Turkish military officers are reported to train Azeri army units. The Turkish government allegedly supplies weapons.

For a provocative look at Russian influence in the war, *see* Thomas Goltz, "Letter from Eurasia: The Hidden Russian Hand," *Foreign Policy*, Fall 1993.

See also, Nikolai Burbyga, "Rossiiskikh Voennykh v Azerbaidzhane prigovorili k smertnoi kazni," *Izvestiya*, Moscow, May 13, 1993, p. 5; "'Dikiye Gusi' vozvrashchayutsya" *Rossiskaya Gazeta*, Moscow, March 5, 1994, p. 3; Jon Auerbach, "Clandestine Russian Force Backs Azeris," *The Boston Globe*, November 22, 1993, p.2; Alexis Rowell, "US army veterans drill Azeris under cover of oil firm," The Observer, (London), November 28, 1993, p.19; Rasit Gurdilek, "Outsiders' motives vary for helping train Azeri troops," *The Washington Times*, February 1, 1994; Alexis Rowell, "US Mercenaries Fight in Azerbaijan," *Covert Action Quarterly*, Spring 1994; "British Mercenaries for Azeri War," *The Independent*, London, January 24, 1994 and "Azeris hire British mercenaries," January 25, 1994.

[226]"Armenia says it shoots down Azeri Aircraft," Reuters, February 18, 1994.

A month later, on March 17, Karabakh forces shot down a Hercules-130 transport plane of the Iranian air force that had wandered over Karabakh airspace. The plane was carrying Iranian embassy personnel from Moscow to Teheran. All on board died.

A full, open accounting of this incident is not known as of this writing. Under the rules of war, the Karabakh Armenians would be duty bound to ascertain the nature of the aircraft before firing. If they did not use every available means to identify the aircraft and still fired, this would constitute a serious violation of humanitarian law.

sixteen missions over Nagorno-Karabakh in 1992; he was shot down on August 20, 1992 over Mardakert Province. He admitted being paid $ 5,000 a month.[227] When he was shot down in 1992, Belichenko was reportedly still on active duty service with the 19th army of the Russian Air Defense Command (PVO).[228]

Most Azerbaijani air attacks against cities in Nagorno-Karabakh seem to be indiscriminate and are intended to demoralize the civilian population.[229] Such attacks against civilians and civilian targets are clearly forbidden under Protocol I, article 51. One pilot shot down by Karabakh Armenian forces stated that the Mig-25 he piloted in bombing raids was not outfitted for precision bombing.[230] Since Nagorno-Karabakh — with help from Armenia — has developed a fairly sophisticated air defense system, bombing raids over Stepanakert are not without risk for pilots.[231] To avoid being shot down, many of these pilots quickly fly over the city and drop their bombs indiscriminately. During Human Rights Watch/Helsinki's April 1994 visit to Nagorno-Karabakh, two air raids against civilian areas in Stepanakert killed eight individuals and wounded thirty-eight. No military targets were located in the vicinity.

While the rules of war do not prohibit the use of mercenaries, they seek to limit their use by denying to such soldiers the status of combatant and prisoner of war.[232] Mercenaries may be tried as common criminals for acts committed in combat, even destroying a legitimate military target or killing an enemy soldier. Mercenaries, when captured, are entitled to the same protection as captured civilians, and may not be summarily executed, tortured, or maltreated. Should the capturing power so elect, mercenaries may be treated as prisoners of war.

The definition of mercenary excludes those who are sent by another state on official duty as a member of the armed forces of that other State and those whose motivation for participation is ideological rather than financial. Protocol I, article 47

---

[227] Vagram Agadzhyan, "Yurii Belichenko: 'Ya soznaval, chto delal." *Nezavisimaya Gazeta*, Moscow, June 26, 1994, p. 3.

[228] Arkadii Zheludkov, "Letchik-Naemnik teper' ne nuzhen nikomu, krome sem'i." *Izvestiya*, Moscow, June 30, 1994, p. 4.

[229] The most egregious use of Azerbaijani air power against civilians occurred in the summer of 1992 and is documented in Human Rights Watch/Helsinki's July 1993 report "Indiscriminate Bombing."

[230] Vargam Agandzhyan, "Yurii Belichenko: 'Ya Soznaval, chto delal." *Nezavisimaya Gazeta*, Moscow, June 21, 1994, p. 3.

[231] Robert Kocharian admitted that the Republic of Armenia supplied anti-aircraft weapons to Nagorno-Karabakh in *Golos Armenii*, Yerevan, February 1, 1994.

[232] Protocol I, article 47 provides:
1. A mercenary shall not have the right to be a combatant or a prisoner of war.

(2), defines a mercenary as any person who:

> (a) is specially recruited locally or abroad in order to fight in an armed conflict;
> (b) does, in fact, take a direct part in the hostilities;
> (c) is motivated to take part in the hostilities essentially by the desire for private gain and, in fact, is promised, by or on behalf of a Party to the conflict, material compensation substantially in excess of that promised or paid to combatants of similar ranks and functions in the armed forces of that Party;
> (d) is neither a national of a Party to the conflict nor a resident of territory controlled by a Party to the conflict;
> (e) is not a member of the armed forces of a Party to the conflict, and
> (f) has not been sent by a State which is not a Party to the conflict on official duty as a member of its armed forces.

VII. THE REPUBLIC OF ARMENIA AS A PARTY TO THE CONFLICT

While Armenia has supported Karabakh forces since the beginning of the conflict, evidence gathered by Human Rights Watch/Helsinki establishes the involvement of the Armenian army as part of its assigned duties in the conflict, especially since December 1993.[233] For much of the time, these forces undertake defensive activities, occupying quiet sectors of the front inside Azerbaijan, relieving more experienced fighters for offensive operations, or guarding lines of communications or rear areas. They are also thrown into battle when needed, especially during Azerbaijan's December 1993-February 1994 offensive.

The government of the Republic of Armenia, however, denies any military involvement in the conflict. Lieutenant General Andreyasyan, then chief of the General Staff of the Armed Forces of Armenia, told Human Rights Watch/Helsinki that no troops under his command fight in Karabakh and that no one on active service is allowed to volunteer in the Karabakh Armenian army.[234] The Armenian Ambassador to the United Nations, Alexander Arzoumanian, stated that, "There are no Armenian troops in Azerbaijan. Of course, there could be citizens of Armenia fighting on a

---

[233]There have been continued reports of official Armenian government military support. In a July 1992 article, *New York Times* reporter Serge Schmemann commented that, "So far Armenia has officially stayed clear of the war, and the Government insists that it is being waged by men from Karabakh and volunteers from Armenia. But it is no mystery where the olive-drab trucks and the tough-looking men thronging the headquarters of the State Directorate of Special Economic Programs — commonly known as the Artsakh Committee — are headed." "In the Caucasus, Ancient Blood feuds threaten to Engulf 2 New Republics," *New York Times*, July 8, 1992, p. 3.

There has always been substantial military support from Armenians living outside of Karabakh during the conflict. Armenians from the diaspora and from the Republic of Armenia — so called fedayeen — have voluntarily been involved in the fighting in Nagorno-Karabakh since the beginning of the conflict. The most famous of them, Monte Melkonian of Vesalia, California, became a legend in Karabakh and Armenia by the time he was killed in fighting in June 1993; an estimated 50,000 people — including the Armenian President, Ter-Petrosyan — attended his funeral in Yerevan. John Cramer, a staff writer for the *Fresno Bee*, spent a week with Melkonian in 1992. Two of his articles give an excellent account of Melkonian and his motivation for fighting in Karabakh. John Cramer, "His life work, Fighting oppression," *Fresno Bee*, September 20, 1992, and "Visalia native dies fighting for Armenian Cause." *Fresno Bee*, June 16, 1993.

[234]Interview, Yerevan, April 11, 1994.

voluntary basis."[235] The evidence, however, outweighs these denials.

Armenian army involvement during the April 1993 Kelbajar offensive seems likely. Many witnesses in Kelbajar before the fall of the city reported seeing artillery fire landing there with a trajectory originating in the Vardenis region of Armenia. Human Rights Watch/Helsinki spoke with two soldiers in the army of the Republic of Armenia (ARA) who while on active duty transported ammunition to Karabakh Armenians fighting in Kelbajar during April 1993.[236] After that offensive, U.N. Secretary-General Boutros Ghali stated that the level of heavy weaponry involved on the Karabakh Armenian side pointed towards Armenian army involvement.[237]

An Armenian prisoner of war told Human Rights Watch/Helsinki that he was drafted in the Armenian army at the military commissariat in the Armenian city of Echmiadzin shortly after his release from jail in June 1993, having served time for petty thievery.[238] He was sent with several soldiers from his Armenian army unit, part of the 83rd Brigade based in Echmiadzin, in August 1993 to Hadrut, in Nagorno-Karabakh, where he guarded military vehicles and storehouses.[239] He was captured at the end of August in an ambush near Fizuli, where he had gone with a detail to retrieve grain.

During Azerbaijan's December 1993 offensive and in fighting in April and May 1994, it appears that military forces — not volunteers — from the Republic of Armenia took part in fighting in Azerbaijan. After setbacks and relatively heavy losses during the initial stages of Azerbaijan's December 1993 offensive, the Armenian leadership in both Stepanakert and Yerevan feared a complete defeat and the possibility of a forced migration of the Karabakh Armenian civilian population. In early February 1994, President Ter-Petrosyan warned that Armenia would involve itself militarily in the conflict should the Karabakh Armenians face "genocide" or forced migration. On April 26, 1994, Ashot Bleyan, an outspoken Armenian parliamentarian, charged the Armenian government with conducting an "undeclared war" in which "only during the last three or four months more than 1,000 Armenian

---

[235]"Armenia denies Involvement in Nagorno-Karabakh." Reuters. February 22, 1994.

[236]Interview, Yerevan, Armenia, April 1994.

[237]Migdalovitz, p. 7.

[238]Armen Terossian, born 1965, Interview, Gobustan Prison, April 3, 1994.

[239]Defensive as well as offensive military duties are included in the term "participating in hostilities", especially where the duties are performed in occupied territory under attack.

youths were killed."[240]

On January 22, 1994, near the village of Chaply in Kelbajar province, Azerbaijani units captured at least two soldiers from the army of the Republic of Armenia and two of Armenian descent from the 127th Division of the Russian army based in Gyumri, Armenia.[241] According to these four soldiers, whom Human Rights Watch/Helsinki interviewed, they were transporting a company of Armenian army soldiers to the front near Kelbajar when they were captured.[242] The men were in a convoy of one "Kamaz 4310" and five "Ural 4320" heavy trucks.[243] They were attacked and captured by Azerbaijani forces after depositing their load of soldiers near the Azeri village of Chaply, Kelbajar province, Azerbaijan. The trucks came from the 127th Division of the Russian army based in Gyumri.

All the men stated that initially they were told by their military commanders that they were going to transport refugees from the Armenian border town of Vardenis, but when they arrived in that city they were ordered by those in command to head to a spot outside of town. There they picked up a company of Armenian army soldiers (approximately 150 men) armed with assault rifles, light machineguns, rocket-propelled grenades, machineguns, and grenade launchers. The men stated that this was the first time that they had made such a trip. The Azerbaijani government alleged these soldiers were from the 555th Independent Motor Rifle Regiment of the ARA (Unit # 59016) and submitted as proof the military identification books (*voennyie bileti*), promotion orders and travel orders captured on January 22, 1994 at Chaply.[244] Then-

---

[240]Snark News Agency, Yerevan, April 26, 1994, in FBIS-SOV-94-082, April 28, 1994. Mr. Blevan is an outspoken opponent of the war. In early 1993, he made an impromptu trip to Baku, for which he was branded a traitor by his colleagues and the Armenian public.

[241]Information Human Rights Watch/Helsinki received indicates that the Russian army is negotiating for the release of the two Russian army soldiers.

[242]Interview, Gobustan Military Prison, Gobustan, Azerbaijan, March 26, 1994 and April 3, 1994. All the interviews were conducted without the presence of prison officials.
    The soldiers captured at Chaply on January 22, 1994 with whom Human Rights Watch/Helsinki spoke were Samvel Badoian, b. 1966, Assistant Commander of the 2nd Department of the Gyumri Military Commissariat, army of Armenia; Ashot Grigorian, Commander of the 4th Section of the Gyumri Military Commissariat, army of Armenia; Stepan Gevorkian, b. 1950, Senior Technician, Transport Company, #11233, 127 Division, Russian army; Razmik Grigorian, b. 1962, mechanic-driver, Transport Company, #11233, 127 Division, Russian army.

[243]These are similar to U.S. army two-and-a-half ton "deuce and a half" trucks.

[244]Statement by Charge d'affaires a.i. of the Permanent Mission of the Azerbaijani Republic to the United Nations, Mr. Yashar Aliyev, February 1994.
    The Soviet army (and now the armies of the various former Soviet republics) did not

Chief of Staff of the Armenian Armed Forces Lieutenant General Andreyasyan denied these soldiers were transporting troops and said that his soldiers were merely transporting supplies and some weapons.[245]

An Armenian army prisoner of war stated that he was captured near the village of Khanlik, Qubatli province of Azerbaijan, on September 19, 1993, while driving a load of telephone communication cable to Karabakh Armenian forces.[246] He was drafted in early 1993 and served in the Independent Communication Unit 32-277 (*Otdel'nyi Chast' Svyazei*) of the Armenian army based in Goris and commanded by Lieutenant Colonel Asadarian. He was not a volunteer.

Another Armenian army prisoner of war captured at the height of the Azerbaijani offensive on January 6, 1994 near the village of (Asagi) Abdurahmanli in Fizuli province was a draftee and did not volunteer for Nagorno-Karabakh.

> I was drafted on December 20, 1992, and was serving in miliary unit 60-369 in Goris under Colonel Grigorian. In the middle of the night of January 5, there was an alarm, and about forty of us were loaded on a Ural truck, given live ammunition, and taken to Abdurahmanli village in Fizuli province. We were in the front line for a few hours, when some more experienced fighters replaced us and we bivouacked in the village. I was ordered to collect firewood, but as I returned to where my comrades were supposed to be I could see them driving away in trucks. I started to run, but ran into an Azeri patrol and was captured.[247]

Outside observers believe that ethnic Armenians either serving in the armed forces of the Republic of Armenia or in the Russian army based in Armenia also service hi-tech SAM anti-aircraft weapons located in Nagorno-Karabakh which defend the enclave from air attack.[248] It is suggested that these soldiers take "leave" and go to Karabakh, or are simply dispatched there.

The Republic of Armenia has even sent members of its police force to perform police duties in occupied Azerbaijan. A police sergeant from the Armenian

---

use dog tags to identify soldiers but small booklets called military tickets (*voennye bileti*).

[245]Interview, Yerevan, April 11, 1994.

[246]Sahak Sosikovich Tamrazian, b. 1961, interview, Gobustan Prison, Gobustan, Azerbaijan, March 26, 1994.

[247]Artak Hacharterian, age 21, resident of Yerevan. Interview, Gobustan Prison, Gobustan, Azerbaijan, March 27, 1994.

[248]Interview, Western diplomat involved in OSCE Minsk Group, June 1994.

border town of Goris told Human Rights Watch/Helsinki he was ordered on September 3, 1993, to set up a control point on the Goris-Qubatli road to prevent looting.[249] Qubatli, an Azerbaijani provincial capital about twenty kilometers from Goris, fell to Karabakh Armenian forces at the end of August 1993. This police officer apparently lost his way in Azerbaijan and was captured.

Human Rights Watch/Helsinki spent two days interviewing Armenian uniformed soldiers at random on the streets of Armenia's capital, Yerevan.[250] Some were truly volunteers, "fedayeen" who had been fighting in Nagorno-Karabakh for four or five years. Others were soldiers from the army of Nagorno-Karabakh on leave in Armenia; they even showed us "NKR voennyi bileti," military identity cards from the NKR Army. But a substantial minority, perhaps 30 percent of the individuals with whom we spoke, were draftees in the ARA who had either fought in Karabakh, had orders to go to Karabakh, or had been "volunteered" for service there — their officers had assembled the troops, explained that the motherland was in danger, and asked for "volunteers."

The heightened Armenian draft requirements also point to Republic of Armenia troop involvement in the conflict.[251] On March 27, 1994, Governmental Decree #129 was passed instituting three- month "refresher training" for men up to forty-five years old.[252] This draft was in addition to normal military conscription in Armenia.

This three-month call-up resulted in "press gang" raids in Armenia.[253] Male Armenian citizens between the ages of twenty-five and forty-five were forbidden to leave the country without special permission. According to a report in the September

---

[249]Interview, Ashot Ambartumian, Gobustan Prison, Gobustan Azerbaijan, April 3, 1994.

[250]All the following interviews took place in Yerevan on April 9 and 10, 1994.

[251]One soldier with whom we spoke was a thirty-seven-year-old unemployed driver who had been caught in Armenian army draft round-ups that occurred in March and April 1994. He said that he would shortly be sent to training and then would be sent to Karabakh.

[252]Interview with Stephen Mirzoyan, head of directorate instituting three month military training, in *Yerkir*, Yerevan, April 6, 1994.

[253]In an April 11, 1994 interview with Human Rights Watch/Helsinki, the chairman of the Ramkavar Party, Ruben Mirzakhanian, complained bitterly of the draft raids. Ramkavar, a liberal, free market party similar to Germany's FDP, is the third largest party in Parliament.
For additional information on spring 1994 draft raids in Armenia, *see also*, Mikhael Danielyan, "Oblavy na Prizyvnikov," *Ekspres Khronika*, Moscow, April 7-14, 1994; "Conscripts Barred from Leaving Armenia," *AIS News Watch*, April 20, 1994; "Forced Conscription as Armenia Shows Strain of War," *AIS News Watch*, May 18, 1994; Alexis Rowell, "Young sacrificed to realise Armenia's old ambition," *Guardian*, London, April 21, 1994.

21, 1994 edition of the Munich daily *Sueddeutsche Zeitung*, a special study of the UNHCR states that those who avoid or refuse military service in Armenia should be given refugee status if they flee the country. Approximately sixty Armenians have fled to the German state of Thueringen to avoid the draft.[254]

Another draftee said that he had been sent to the Lachin area of Azerbaijan in April 1993 and to the Omar pass region of Kelbajar province during operations to recapture it in January-February 1994. He had been wounded in fighting and was recuperating in Yerevan. One soldier reported that he was on active duty in the Armenian army, but had volunteered to fight in Karabakh. He stated that half his unit (around 600 men) were stationed in Kelbajar province.

We also spoke with Armenian army soldiers traveling on buses into Nagorno-Karabakh from Armenia. On a single day, Sunday, April 17, 1994, Human Rights Watch/Helsinki counted five "Ikarus" buses full of Armenian Army soldiers entering Nagorno-Karabakh, holding an estimated 300 men in all.[255] Three buses were on the Lachin-Stepanakert road, one was stopped in the Azerbaijani town of Lachin, and one was broken down with a flat tire outside of the Armenian border town of Goris.

We spoke with several soldiers from the bus in Goris. All were armed with new AK-47 assault rifles. Some said they were draftees. Their officer at first denied they were headed to Karabakh, then admitted it, arguing that "Karabakh is Armenian land and had to be defended."[256] The day before, four such buses pulled into Stepanakert.

Other Western journalists leaving Karabakh later in the week reported seeing eight buses full of Armenian Army soldiers entering Karabakh from Armenia and received similar information talking with these soldiers.[257] Other reporters have

---

[254]"Uno Stellt Sich Hinter Wehrdienst Verweigerer" September 21, 1994 *Sueddeutsche Zeitung*, Munich, p. 9.

[255]Produced in Hungary, the "Ikarus" bus served as the mainstay of the Soviet bloc bus fleet. The bus we saw could hold an estimated sixty men.

The week of April 10-18, 1994, witnessed heavy fighting along the whole front, especially near Agdam and Mardakert, and two air raids against Stepanakert. Most mornings artillery barrages from Agdam and Mardakert were clearly audible in Stepanakert. Karabakh losses for the week were extremely heavy, with possibly as many as one hundred killed. The week ended with the Armenian capture of the strategically important villages Talish and Chailou in Mardakert Province.

[256]Interview, Goris, Armenia, April 17, 1994.

[257]Christopher Pala, *The Washington Times* and AFP.

encountered similar stories while in Armenia and Nagorno-Karabakh.[258]

The saddest testament to Armenian government involvement in the conflict is Yeriblur Military Cemetery in Armenia's capital, Yerevan. The cemetery serves as the main military cemetery for Yerevan, though dead from Karabakh are buried throughout Armenia. It has an official military honor guard.[259]

When we visited the cemetery in early April, we were told that 420 military men were buried there. From our calculations based on the tombstones, approximately 25 to 30 percent were buried in 1994, a majority of them of draft age (birthdates from 1973-1975). The Republic of Armenia is not involved in any internal conflict and in no other international conflict, aside from that with Azerbaijan. A second visit to Yeriblur military cemetery ten days later unfortunately revealed about thirty new graves.[260]

By coincidence, our taxi driver told us that his relative, Robert Gevorkian, a colonel in a Ministry of Internal Affairs unit stationed within sight of the cemetery near the airport, was buried there. He showed us the grave, and told us, "He wasn't a volunteer, but a colonel in the MVD forces [Armenian Ministry of the Interior Troops]. He had been there [Nagorno-Karabakh] several times before with his unit. They got called over when things got hot in Karabakh."[261]

As a matter of law, Armenian army troop involvement in Azerbaijan makes Armenia a party to the conflict and makes the war an international armed conflict, as between the government of Armenia and Azerbaijan.[262]

---

[258]Steve Levine, "Azerbaijan Throws Raw Recruits into Battle," *The Washington Post*, April 21, 1994. Levine encountered a convoy of five buses outside of Yerevan carrying Armenian army recruits. They men reported they were headed to the city of Horadiz in Azerbaijan, a key point of the front line presently in Azeri control.

[259]Human Rights Watch/Helsinki viewed video tape shot by a Western journalist on March 11, 1994 that showed an Armenian military unit burying with full military honors two of their comrades killed near Fizuli, Azerbaijan. The commander of the unit, however, claimed the men were volunteers.

[260]Human Rights Watch/Helsinki visited Yeriblur on April 9 and April 19, 1994.

[261]Interview, April 19, 1994; see Raymond Bonner, "War, Blockade, and Poverty Strangling Armenia," *The New York Times*, April 16, 1994. Bonner reported the participation in the conflict of soldiers from the Armenian Ministry of the Interior.

[262]*See* Appendix A, International Law.

VIII. BLOCKADES AND EMBARGOES

Lines of communication and transportation between Armenia and oil-producing Azerbaijan have been interrupted since 1989, at first sporadically, and by 1991 completely. Land routes to Nagorno-Karabakh were closed until Karabakh Armenian forces seized Lachin on May 17, 1992, an action that linked their enclave with Armenia proper.

The Armenian government charges that Azerbaijan has imposed a blockade on Armenia even though it is not party to the conflict; Azerbaijan counters that it merely has placed an embargo on trade with a nation with which it considers itself in a state of armed conflict, and is under no obligation to trade with Armenia. Armenia, a land-locked country, borders Georgia, Turkey, Azerbaijan, and Iran.

Presently, the main route from Armenia to the outside world runs through strife-torn Georgia. However, banditry makes travel dangerous. On March 2, a rail bridge over the Khram river in Georgia was sabotaged, putting Armenia's only rail link with the outside world out of service for several days.[263] This is not an infrequent occurrence.

Humanitarian goods came sporadically through Turkey, Armenia's western neighbor, but in early February 1993 an agreement was reached between Armenia and Turkey to increase the shipment of aid from France and the United States through Turkey.[264] Turkey cut all routes to Armenia in April 1993 after the Karabakh Armenian army — with alleged support from the Russian and Armenian armies — seized Kelbajar province in Azerbaijan.[265]

The most telling indicator of the toll the war and the embargo has had on life in Armenia is the willingness of people to leave it: between 300,000-800,000 Armenians left the country last year, an estimated 20 percent of Armenia's population

---

[263]"Blast cuts Armenia's rail links with Other States," Reuters, March 2, 1994.

The fighting and unrest in Chechnya has disrupted rail and road transport to Azerbaijan, and in late December 1994, the Russian government closed the border between Azerbaijan and the Russian Federation. In late autumn, Turkey had to rush emergency shipments of grain to Azerbaijan.

[264]Mary Curtius, "Armenia says Turkey has agreed to open supply routes for aid," *The Boston Globe*, February 5, 1993.

[265]According to State Department officials, Turkey justifies its refusal to allow the transit of aid to Armenia by pointing to U.S. cut off of Freedom Support Aid to Azerbaijan. Turkish politicians, they claim, must also listen to the electorate.

of close to three million.[266] The country is dependent on imports for two-thirds of its food and most of its energy requirements.[267] Bread, the main staple, is rationed.

Conditions are even worse during the winter because of energy shortages. Even during the best of times heat and light are in short supply, but during 1993, Armenia met only 30 percent of its energy needs.[268] A gas pipeline passing through the Marneuli region of Georgia — an area populated by ethnic Azeris — is regularly blown up; in January 1994 it was sabotaged three times.[269] Despite Western objections, Armenia intends in early 1995 to open the Metzamor nuclear reactor closed after the 1988 earthquake. Russia will provide the financing. On September 6, 1994, Russia's First Deputy Atomic Energy Minister Lev Ryabyev signed a protocol with Armenian Deputy Prime Minister Vigen Chitechyan granting Armenia a loan of 60 billion rubles (US $30 million) to reopen the reactor.[270] Armenian Deputy Prime Minister of Energy Stephen Tashjian commented that, "At this point Armenia has no option, just no option [but to open the reactor]."[271] In general, the Armenian economy is devasted because of the energy shortage brought on by Azerbaijan's energy embargo.

The Nakhichevan Autonomous Republic, part of Azerbaijan and populated by Azeris but separated from Azerbaijan by the Zangezur region of Armenia, also

[266]Sergei Bablumyan, "Emigratsiya iz Armenii priobrela kharakter natsional'nogo Bedstviya." *Izvestiya.* Moscow, April 22, 1994, p. 3; RFE/RL Daily Report, June 27, 1994. Some may leave temporarily, such as in winter.

[267]According to Armen Darbinian, Vice Minister of Economy of Armenia, Armenia grows 300,000 tons of wheat and imports another [one] million tons; 480,000 tons are used to bake bread, a food staple that the government subsidizes. He added that Armenia must import all its sugar and ninety percent of its milk products, up from sixty percent during Soviet times. With the exception of grain, Georgia takes thirty percent of all goods shipped to its territory to Armenia. Interview, Yerevan, Armenia, April 12, 1994.

[268]AZG, Yerevan, January 27, 1994.

[269]"Wichtige Gas-Pipeline nach Armenian gesprengt." *Sueddeutsche Zeitung,* Munich, January 13, 1994, p.6.

[270]Robert Eksuzyan, "Armenian nuclear plant due to reopen in early 1995." Reuters, September 8, 1994.

[271]Raymond Bonner, "War, Blockade, and Poverty 'Strangling' Armenia." *The New York Times,* April 16, 1994.

suffers because of economic dislocation.[272] Since June 1992 the region has been blockaded also: Azerbaijan alleges that Armenia blockades the Azeri enclave, cutting it from the rest of Azerbaijan, while Armenian officials claim that Azerbaijan's blockade of Armenia is the cause of Nakhichevan's woes because rail lines that run to the Azeri enclave inside Armenia originate in Azerbaijan and are thus cut off.[273] Likewise, Nakhichevan suffers from Armenia's energy shortfall. According to Hasan Zeynalov, Representative of the Nakhichevan Autonomous Republic in Azerbaijan, the 300,000 inhabitants of Nakhichevan receive only about fifteen percent of the required fuel and medicine.[274] The heavily mechanized agricultural sector, where about seventy percent of the population is employed, suffers accordingly. Only twelve of thirty factories operate on any level at all, and thirty percent of the labor force is idle. Electric lines run to Turkey, but the Kurdish PKK rebels in Turkey sometimes blow up the transmission towers, interrupting the supply.[275] Some supplies come in from Turkey over the *Umit Koprusu*, the Bridge of Hope, and from Iran. Mr. Zeynalov pointed out, however, that before Karabakh Armenian forces seized the Azerbaijani provinces south of Karabakh, goods could be brought closer to Nakhichevan and then transshipped through Iran; now that these provinces are in Armenian hands, goods coming to Nakhichevan from Azerbaijan must take a much longer and circuitous route. Mr. Zeynalov also asserted that the blockade of Nakhichevan started in 1988 and 1989, when trains entering the enclave were attacked.

In Nakhichevan the Adventist Development and Relief Agency (ADRA), the only Western humanitarian organization to have a presence in this enclave, disburses twenty kilogram food packages to 20,000 families a month. The United States government pays for the food parcels, which are shipped from Mersin, Turkey over the Bridge of Hope. According to an ADRA official who is stationed in Nakhichevan,

> the blockade has totally ruined the economy. Agriculture is at a
> standstill, people are eating their seeds. Irrigation also collapsed —

---

[272] The Nakhichevan enclave is bounded by Armenia to the north and east and Iran to the west and south. It also shares a tiny, ten kilometer border with Turkey. Under the 1921 Treaty of Kars, Turkey is a guarantor power for Nakhichevan.

[273] Human Rights Watch/Helsinki, "Indiscriminate Bombing", p. 7.

In May/June 1992 there was intense fighting near Sadarak, in northern Nakhichevan. Armenian forces seized the small Azeri enclave of Kyarki, just north of Nakhichevan. The area is part of Azerbaijan but lies inside Armenia.

[274] Interview, March 24, 1994. The following information is from Mr. Zeynalov, unless otherwise stated.

[275] The PKK, the Kurdish Workers Party, is a separatist Kurdish rebel group that has been fighting a guerilla war against the Turkish government in southeastern Turkey since 1984.

no spare parts for the pumps. Everything is deforested. You really have to go up in the hills before you see trees that haven't been turned into stumps. There is constant shooting and sniping across the whole length of the border. Both sides do it. Some of my drivers are terrified to take parcels to some remote villages.[276]

Small kitchen gardens and subsidized prices for bread prevent real undernourishment.

Human Rights Watch/Helsinki does not consider either blockade to be a violation of the prohibition on using starvation of the civilian population as means of warfare or combat.[277] In neither case is the requisite intention to starve civilians as a method of warfare evident. We will continue to monitor the war to determine whether either party steps over the line.

---

[276]Interview, Baku, April 4, 1994, with Marty Phillips and Dwight Woods of the Adventist Development and Relief Agency.

[277]*See* Appendix A, International Law.

IX. U.S. POLICY

The United States has two Karabakh policies: one originating on Capitol Hill, the other in the White House. While the State Department has attempted to play the role, in the words of former Ambassador-at-Large Strobe Talbott, of "an honest broker in the conflict," condemning displacement of civilians and human rights abuses by both sides, Congress has adopted a decidedly pro-Armenian position and has hardly criticized Armenian human rights abuses.

Congress' Karabakh policy seems a captive of U.S. domestic politics. In Section 907a of the October 1992 Freedom Support Act, Congress denied all aid to the Azerbaijan government unless it respected international human rights standards, abandoned its blockade of Armenia, ceased its use of force against Karabakh and Armenia, and sought a peaceful solution to the conflict.[278] Thus, for example, no aid can be given to improve an intensive care unit in a hospital in Azerbaijan because the hospital is state-owned. Azerbaijan alone among all the former Soviet republics was denied aid, while Armenia became the highest per capita aid recipient. On June 16, 1994, the Senate Appropriations Committee allocated $75 million in aid for Armenia for FY 1995 while preventing any loosening of Section 907.[279] To date, U.S. aid to Armenia totals $335 million dollars.[280]

U.S. humanitarian aid does find its way to Azerbaijan through private volunteer organizations. According to the State Department, the U.S. government disbursed about twenty-five million dollars of humanitarian aid to Azerbaijan's citizens through private volunteer organizations since 1993.

Other Congressional legislative initiatives have been principally directed against Azerbaijan. In February 1993, House Resolution 86, introduced by Rep. David Bonior of Michigan, would have condemned Azerbaijan for its blockade of Armenia and called on it to work towards a peaceful resolution to the conflict.[281] The bill did not pass.

There was strong Congressional opposition to bill H.R. 3765, one provision of which would have lifted aid restrictions to the Azerbaijani government. The bill was introduced by Rep. Lee Hamilton of Indiana, Chairman of House Foreign Affairs Committee, in early 1994 at the request of the Clinton administration. In March 1994,

---

[278]Migdalovitz, p. 15.

[279]*AIS News Watch*, June 22, 1994, p. 1.

[280]A.D. Horne, "Armenian Leader Argues for Russian Truce Force," *Washington Post*, August 11, 1994, p. 24.

[281]Migdalovitz, p.16.

Representative Dick Swett, Democrat of New Hampshire, argued against the proposal, but his facts were wrong: "I strongly urge that you [Rep. Hamilton] retain the prohibition on American assistance to Azerbaijan until Azerbaijani troops cease their occupation of Nagorno-Karabakh and stop their aggressive actions against the Republic of Armenia."[282] In 1994, however, Azerbaijan did not control, let alone occupy Karabakh; indeed, Karabakh Armenian forces controlled all Azerbaijani provinces to the south, west, and east of the enclave after having evicted an estimated 500,000 Azeris from these territories the year before.

The State Department has adopted a more balanced approach, usually condemning both sides for actions that tend to widen the conflict or cause civilian population dislocation. For example, the State Department condemned Karabakh Armenian offensives against Azerbaijan in 1993 as well as Azerbaijan's use of Afghan mujahideen. It condemned the July 1993 Karabakh Armenian seizure of Agdam, stating that "[it] cannot be justified on the grounds of legitimate self-defense."[283] As mentioned above, the administration has sought the repeal of the Freedom Support Act restrictions on aid to Azerbaijan.

Administration policy remains fully committed to the OSCE Minsk Group peace negotiations and has sought to counter a solely "Russian" solution to the conflict.[284] The administration is not opposed, however, to substantial Russian participation in a peacekeeping force. On the occasion of Armenian President Ter-Petrosyan's August 1994 official visit to Washington, President Clinton commented that, "'the United States would not object' to the Russian troops' presence 'if the parties agree to it and there were clear [OSCE] safeguards so that we had the right sort of oversight." [285] In early September 1994, United States U.N. representative Madeleine Albright underscored this policy, stating that the United States was not against Russian peacekeeping missions in the "near abroad," commenting that "Russia has the resources, direct interests and the leadership required to help resolve the problem in this region."[286] She added that this was not the ideal situation and that the "burden of proof is on Russia to prove its commitment to accepted international principles to the sovereignty of the newly independent states and to adopting a neutral stance in ethnic

---

[282]Armenian National Committee of America press release. March 31, 1994.

[283]Migdalovitz, p. 7.

[284]John Maresca, former U.S. special negotiator for Nagorno-Karabakh, has called for repealing Section 907a of the Freedom Support Act. *The Washington Post* has called 907a "raw ethnic politics."

[285]A.D. Horne, August 11, 1994, p. 24.

[286]"US approves of role of Russian troops in CIS States," *Financial Times*, London, September 7, 1994, p. 16.

conflicts."[287] At the December 1994 Budapest OSCE summit, Secretary Christopher commented that, ". . . In connection with Karabakh we hope and expect there'll be worked out here. . . an arrangement under which both the Russian and OSCE efforts in Nagorno-Karabakh can then be brought effectively into play."[288]

---

[287]"Albright says world watching Russian peacekeepers." Reuters. September 6, 1994.

[288]Jonathan Clayton, "Russia blocks deal on Karabakh peace force." Reuters, December 4, 1994.

X. PEACE NEGOTIATIONS

OSCE MINSK GROUP

Cease-fires and peace attempts have been short-lived in the Karabakh conflict, but a shaky cease-fire worked out by the Russian government has held since May 1994. At present, two main bodies conduct negotiations to end the fighting in Nagorno-Karabakh: the OSCE Minsk Group and the Russian government. Many observers believe Russia's peacemaking efforts conflict with — and even undermine those of the OSCE Minsk Group — especially over the issue of peacekeeping and monitoring forces. Russia is also a member of the Minsk Group.

The eleven-member OSCE Minsk Group was formed in the summer of 1992 and is named after Belorussia's capital because a peace conference was scheduled to be held there.[289] Other members of the Minsk Group include Armenia, Azerbaijan, Turkey, France, Germany, Italy, Sweden, the Czech Republic, Belarus, the United States, and "interested parties in Nagorno-Karabakh." The Minsk Group's present chairman is the Swedish diplomat Anders Bjurner.[290]

The goals of the Minsk Group include bringing all interested parties — including Karabakh Armenians — to the negotiating table, achieving a cease-fire with OSCE-sponsored international monitoring, the lifting of all blockades, aiding refugees and displaced persons, and ultimately negotiating the status of Nagorno-Karabakh.[291]

The Minsk Group has worked out various timetables of "Urgent Measures" to end the fighting, but both Azerbaijan and Nagorno-Karabakh have rejected the plans at various times. On several occasions Minsk Group recommendations have served as the basis for U.N. Resolutions; otherwise the U.N. is not involved in conflict mediation.

On December 6, 1994, after serious disagreement between the OSCE and Russia was overcome, the OSCE at its Budapest summit decided to send a 3,000-strong OSCE multinational peacekeeping force to Nagorno-Karabakh. It was also

---

[289] Human Rights Watch/Helsinki,"Indiscriminate Bombing," p.8. The peace conference was never held in Minsk. Russia is a member of the Minsk Group.

[290] The previous chairman was the Swede Jan Eliasson, who replaced the Italian diplomat Mario Raffaelli in December 1993.

[291] John Maresca, "War in the Caucasus: A Proposal for Settlement of the Conflict over Nagorno-Karabakh," United States Institute for Peace, Washington, July 1, 1994, p. 4.

decided that Russia and Sweden would jointly chair the Minsk Group.[292] This is the first time the OSCE has taken on a peacekeeping role in an armed conflict. Although several OSCE members such as Turkey, Russia, Ukraine, and several Central European countries agreed to send troops, the actual composition of the force must be worked out.[293] Russia had earlier insisted on providing most of the troops for the force, but it was reportedly agreed that no one state could contribute more than thirty percent of the troops.[294] The deployment of a peacekeeping force ultimately depends on turning the May 1994 cease-fire into a permanent truce. The U.S. Security Council must also approve sending a peacekeeping force.

RUSSIAN POLICY AND PEACE NEGOTIATIONS

Although Russia has played a large role in peace negotiations, many doubt its intentions because of its obvious strategic interests in the Transcaucasus, its desire to base troops in Azerbaijan, where at present no Russian troops are stationed, and its past history of involvement in the conflict. The OSCE's December 1994 decision to send a multinational peacekeeping force to Karabakh was worked out only after serious, high-level negotiations between Russian and other OSCE members, such as the United States. Earlier Russian plans for peacekeepers envisioned a clear Russian command role, which the OSCE Minsk Group rejected.

Russia has had a mediating role since September 1991, when Russian President Boris Yeltsin and Kazakhstan's leader Nursultan Nazarbaev worked out an agreement that came to nought when a helicopter carrying Russian and Azerbaijani officials crashed.[295] Russia's mediation increased after Heidar Aliyev came to power in Azerbaijan via a military coup in June 1993. President Yeltsin's envoy to the region, Vladimir Kazimirov, plays a large role along with Defense Minister Grachev. In the past, both had been critical of OSCE's initiatives because it does not have troops to send to Karabakh to serve as peacekeepers, though this no longer seems the case with

---

[292] Paris AFP, December 6, 1994, FBIS-WEV-94-234, December 6, 1994, p. 1.

Final details of the peacekeeping force were to be worked out at an OSCE conference on January 9, 1995, but the fighting in Chechnya may change that.

[293]"Peacekeeping troops may go to Karabakh next year," Reuters, December 7, 1994.

[294]Richard Balmforth, "OSCE approves peacekeeping force for Karabakh," Reuters, December 6, 1994.

[295]Elizabeth Fuller, "Russia's Diplomatic Offensive in the Transcaucasus," *RFE/RL Research Report*, October 1,1993, p. 32.

There are reports that the helicopter was shot down by machine gun fire from an Armenian-populated village in Karabakh.

the OSCE's December 1994 decision to deploy a force.

In September 1993, Russia brokered talks in Moscow between the Azerbaijani officials and representatives of the self-proclaimed Nagorno-Karabakh "Republic."[296] The most recent two cease-fires are the result of Russian-sponsored negotiations. Russian Defense Minister Pavel Grachev and Deputy Defense Minister Georgii Kondratev worked out cease-fire agreements on February 18, 1994, and on May 16, 1994.[297]

John Maresca, former U.S. Ambassador to the OSCE and special U.S. negotiator for Nagorno-Karabakh, has stated that,

> At first, Russia fully supported the Minsk Group. But in 1993 Russia reactivated its earlier independent mediation effort. . . . The reason was clear: Russia wished to reestablish its dominance in the region and to exclude outsiders, namely the US and Turkey. Russia wants to dominate Armenia and Azerbaijan for a number of reasons. Most obviously, Moscow would like to reestablish control of the former Soviet frontier with Turkey and Iran, and to share in Azerbaijan's oil riches. To accomplish these aims, Russia has been pressuring Azerbaijan to accept the reentry of Russian troops as a separation force and as border guards, as to give Russia a share of the oil concessions being developed by Western companies. For leverage, the Russians have used an implicit but dramatic threat: If Azerbaijan does not comply, Russia will step up its backing for Armenia (Russian troops are already stationed there), with disastrous military results for the Azeris.[298]

Grachev's May 16, 1994, cease-fire negotiations, for example, coincided with a visit to the region by former OSCE Minsk Group Chairman Eliasson; however, no OSCE Minsk Group representative was present at the Grachev meeting in spite of Azerbaijani requests.[299] The Grachev Plan of May 16 called for only Russian officers to head the forty-nine observer posts and for 1,800 CIS (mostly Russian) troops under General Kondratev to separate the hostile forces, a marked difference from the mixed

---

[296]Fuller, 1993, p. 34.

[297]See, "Moscow sends envoy to secure Karabakh Ceasefire," Reuters, March 1, 1994; John Lloyd, "Peace hopes rise in Karabakh conflict," *Financial Times*, London, February 11, 1994.

[298]John J. Maresca, "Agony of Indifference in Nagorno-Karabakh," *The Christian Science Monitor*, Boston, June 27, 1994, p. 19.

[299]Elizabeth Fuller, "The Karabakh Mediation Process: Grachev versus the OSCE," *RFE/RL Research Report*, June 10, 1994, pp. 13-14.

OSCE force now to be sent in which no one country will contribute more than thirty percent of the forces. The OSCE proposal at the time had called for the observer posts to monitor both the cease-fire and the conduct of peacekeeping forces.[300] A Western diplomat involved in the peace process commented that, "The Russians are still very unwilling to have people oversee their actions or to have international forces operating in the former Soviet Union."[301]

At a September 1994 Prague meeting of the OSCE's Committee of Senior Officials, serious complaints were voiced at Russia's Karabakh peace initiatives outside of the OSCE's Minsk Group.[302] Complaints included Russia's initiating a September 8, 1994, Azerbaijan-Armenia Summit in Moscow without informing the OSCE; snubbing a OSCE Minsk Group meeting; demanding a CIS/Russian peacekeeping force in Karabakh rather than a OSCE multinational force. The committee called for "the harmonization" and "coordination" of mediation activities.

Azerbaijan was extremely suspicious of the deployment in Nagorno-Karabakh and Azerbaijan of a Russian-only peacekeeping and monitoring force without strong OSCE or international supervision; the Azerbaijani Parliament erupted in protest at the idea. Azerbaijani President Aliyev, who in the past criticized the OSCE Minsk Group, rejected the Russian proposal and awaited the OSCE plan.[303] On a June 11, 1994, trip to Azerbaijan, Grachev convinced Aliyev to participate in a unified air defense system for Transcaucasia and to allow Russia to continue using a strategic radar system at Gabala in northern Azerbaijan, but was unable to get the Azerbaijani president to sign the cease-fire agreement allowing Russian peacekeepers.[304] In August of this year, the Azerbaijani Ambassador to the United States, Hafiz Pashayev, stated that, "We don't have any foreign troops in our country,

---

[300]*Ibid.* General Grachev has also adopted a very heavy-handed approach to the negotiations, stating that, "If you want me to be your mediator, by all means, but if there are other opinions about Russian peacekeepers — keep killing yourself further, we won't waste our time and money. . . . What I suggest will be agreed on, and without any ulterior motives. . . . You can be sure, if I deploy our troops there, there will be a second step, and a third, and all the rest." Liana Minasyan, "Pavel Grachev: Kak Ya predlozhu, Tak i Zatverdim." *Nezavisimaya Gazeta,* Moscow, May 17, 1994, p. 1. He referred to others steps, such as a withdrawal from occupied territory, lifting of blockades, and freeing of prisoners.

[301]Nicholas Doughty, "U.S. raises fears with Russian peacekeeping line." Reuters, September 21, 1994.

[302]RFE/RL Daily Report, September 20, 1994.

[303]RFE/RL Daily Report, May 18, 1994.

[304]RFE/RL Daily Report, June 13, 1994; "Russia's Grachev says Azeri Talks successful." Reuters, June 11, 1993.

and we don't want any."[305]

Armenia, on the other hand, welcomed Russian peacekeepers, but was also enthusiastic about the OSCE plan to send the 3,000-strong multinational force. On an official visit to the United States, Armenian President Ter-Petrosyan stated that, "Only Russia is prepared to contribute its forces for peacekeeping purposes. . . . I have no choice . . . . But I'm confident that the officials who are in power in Russia do not have the goal of re-establishing Russia's empire."[306]

---

[305]Steven Greenhouse. "Armenia Says It Would Welcome Russian Peacekeeping Offer." *The New York Times*, August 12, 1994.

[306]Greenhouse, August 12, 1994.

XI. RUSSIAN WEAPONRY, SOURCES OF ARMS, AND LIMITS ON NEW ACQUISITIONS

For more than seventy years, the Soviet Union served as the "arsenal of communism," producing and stockpiling huge quantities of all types of weapons. In an August 1992 interview, Vagan Shirkhanian, a military adviser to the Armenian president, commented that, "the supply of weapons will last for years, thank God, the former USSR produced so many."[307] The conflict in Nagorno-Karabakh quickly outgrew its early "Karabakh Armenian villager with a hunting rifle" stage, and today modern tanks and armored personnel carriers, heavy artillery and rockets, and light weapons of all types stock the arsenals of Azerbaijani, Karabakh Armenian, and Armenian forces. In short, cheap weapons are readily available to combatants.

Such unregulated and often criminally-negligent arms trades provide the means for serious human rights violation such as those committed in the fighting in Karabakh. These armaments — some transferred legally to the Soviet successor states, some stolen, and some sold by corrupt military officers or by armament factories hungry for customers — have fueled conflicts throughout the former Soviet empire and increased the toll of civilian suffering.

The influx of weapons into the conflict has numerous sources, some legal, some illegal. Soviet army stocks provided an initial source. The Soviet Seventh Army stationed in Armenia and the Fourth Army in Azerbaijan both had large stockpiles of weapons that quickly ended up in the hands of combatants on both sides through raids on arsenals and the illegal sale of weapons by sergeants and officers of the Soviet Army.[308] In March 1992, Armenian irregulars killed two Russian soldiers and took hostage another in a raid for weapons on a military base in Artik, Armenia.[309] When the Russian 366th Motor Rifle Regiment based in Stepanakert was pulled out in the spring of 1992, it left all of its weapons to the Karabakh Armenians.[310]

---

[307]Liana Minasyan, "Zapasov Oruzhiya Khavtit na mnogo let." *Nezavisimaya Gazeta*, Moscow, August 26, 1992, p. 8.

[308]Dmitrii Trenin and Vadim Makarenko, "Chto delat' armii, kogda krugom idet voina," *Novoye Vremya*, Moscow, No. 21, 1992, p. 21.

[309]Steven Erlanger, "Caucasus War: Any Role for Moscow?", *The New York Times*, March 13, 1992, p.3. In a press conference held in March 1992, then-Vice-President Alexander Rutskoi stated that 2,000 weapons and 60 vehicles had been seized since January 1992.

[310]Interview with Robert Kocharian, Chairman of the Defense Committee of Nagorno-Karabakh, in *Golos Armenii*, Yerevan, February 1, 1994. The interview initially appeared in the Moscow paper, *Segodnya*, No. 12, 1994. During 1992 there were also mysterious fires and explosions at Soviet Army ammunition dumps outside of Baku and Agdam in Azerbaijan and

Azerbaijan and Armenia both received a share of the Soviet military arsenal under the May 1992 Treaty of Tashkent. Under this agreement — which received international confirmation in the July 1992 Treaty on Conventional Forces in Europe — Azerbaijan and Armenia each received from the former arsenal of the Soviet Union 220 tanks, 220 armored personnel carriers, and 285 artillery pieces.[311] They are prohibited from exceeding these levels, and each year every signatory of the CFE treaty must give a copy of its weapons inventory and dislocation of weapons to the OSCE in Vienna. These inventories are than exchanged among the signatories.

Both sides accuse each other of violating the limits set in these agreements: Azerbaijan claims that Armenia supplies the Karabakh forces with weapons and munitions, pointing to captured equipment allegedly bearing serial numbers from Armenian stockpiles.[312] Armenia alleges that Azerbaijan purchased large quantities of weapons abroad, including tanks from Ukraine.[313] Both allegations seem to have some truth. According to NATO officials, 2,000 tanks, APCs, and artillery pieces covered under CFE are missing and unaccounted for from Russian, Armenian, Georgian, Azerbaijani, and Moldovan inventories.[314] Reports indicate that the ARA is chronically short of equipment.[315] Several Western embassies reportedly complained to the Azerbaijani government concerning its arms purchases abroad. On July 20, 1994, Azerbaijani presidential adviser on military affairs Nureddin Sadykhov stated that Azerbaijan was considering asking for permission to increase its weapons levels under CFE given that it has twice the population of Armenia and is considerably larger geographically.[316]

---

near Yerevan, Armenia: some informed sources believe these explosions were set to cover up illegal large-scale weapons transfers.

[311]Douglas Clarke. "The Russian Military and the CFE Treaty." *Radio Free Europe/Radio Liberty Research Report*, October 22, 1993, p. 39.

[312]Vagif I. Sadykhov, Head of the Political-Military Affairs Section of the Ministry of Foreign Affairs, Azerbaijan, made these allegations at a meeting with Human Rights Watch/Helsinki in March 1994. He later supplied a video tape of tanks with serial numbers that purportedly come from Armenian stockpiles.

[313]Alexander Zhilin. "Tanks used in Karabakh may be Ukrainian." *Moscow News*, September 17, 1993; Yerevan Armenia Radio First in FBIS-SOV-93-174, September 10, 1993, p. 63.

[314]Sally Jacobsen. "35,000 Tanks, Artillery pieces destroyed in Europe under Arms Accord," AP, November 30, 1994.

[315]Elizabeth Fuller. "Paramilitary Forces Dominate Fighting in Transcaucasia." *RFE/RL Research Report*, June 18, 1993, p. 77.

[316]RFE/RL Daily Report, 21 July 1994.

The Russian government reportedly handed the CFE Consultative Group in Vienna a note alleging that Azerbaijani armament purchases during autumn 1993 exceeded CFE limitations by 116 tanks, 103 artillery pieces, and 727 APCs.

There are two other important sources of weapons: purchases on favorable credit terms from Russia and captures during combat. Russia liberally supplies both sides with weapons, reportedly on easy credit terms.[317] In a May 17, 1994 Moscow press conference, Russian Defense Minister Pavel Grachev stated that both CIS and non-CIS states were supplying arms in the conflict.[318] During the height of the Azerbaijani offensive that began in December 1993, individuals from the Russian Ministry of Defense reportedly regularly called Karabakh authorities to inquire about the military situation and weapons needs, and sent large weapons shipments through the Lachin corridor.[319] A Western diplomat active in the OSCE Minsk Group talks told Human Rights Watch/Helsinki that at peak periods roughly forty Russian transport planes landed at Yerevan's airport daily. The Karabakh Armenians have managed to capture large numbers of tanks and armored personnel carriers from the Azerbaijani army in battle, so-called "trofei," or trophies.[320]

Weapons used in the conflict come from the standard Soviet arsenal and were initially designed for Soviet action against NATO armies. BMP Type 1 and 2 armored personnel carriers armed with a variety of light cannons and machine guns and T-72 main battle tanks armed with 125mm cannons are widely used. BM-21, "Grad" rockets also find wide deployment, and their misuse has led to widespread civilian casualties. Heavy artillery and mortars are used by both sides, but are particularly useful for the numerically smaller Karabakh Armenian forces. During heavy fighting in April 1994, heavy, lengthy barrages in the Agdam region were clearly audible in Stepanakert.[321] Mines are also widely used by both sides.

Azerbaijan also has employed air power, mostly SU-25 ground attack fighters, in a targeted manner to support ground troops as well as indiscriminately

---

[317]Felix Corley, "Nagorno-Karabakh-An Eyewitness Account," *Jane's Intelligence Review*, April 1994, p. 165.

[318]RFE/RL Daily Report, May 18, 1994.

[319]Interview with Tigran Xmalian, Political Analyst, Armenian Assembly of America, Yerevan, Armenia, April 1994.

Mr. Xmalian had worked as a war correspondent in Karabakh for the Russian TV program "Vesti". He spoke with Human Rights Watch/Helsinki as a private citizen, not as a representative of the Armenian Assembly. He claimed to have seen some of the weapons shipments passing through the Lachin corridor.

[320]They even have a tank repair station in Stepanakert to repair captured military booty.

[321]Human Rights Watch/Helsinki representatives were in Nagorno-Karabakh from April 13-April 18.

against population centers in Nagorno-Karabakh and in Armenia. Many observers reported that Azerbaijan used ground support aircraft widely during its December 1993 offensive. Azerbaijan is also reported to use ground attack helicopters for tactical air support.

APPENDIX A: INTERNATIONAL LAW

The enclave of Nagorno-Karabakh is part of the territory of Azerbaijan as that republic was internationally recognized when it became independent of the USSR in 1991. The enclave is surrounded on all sides by territory of Azerbaijan. Although Nagorno-Karabakh has declared its independence, this has not been recognized by the international community, nor is it likely to be. Prior to the war approximately 180,000 individuals lived in Nagorno-Karabakh. Nagorno-Karabakh has an area of roughly 1,700 square miles.

This armed conflict is an example of an "internationalized" internal or non-international armed conflict, that is, a civil war characterized by the intervention of the armed forces of other states on behalf of rebels.[322] The Republic of Armenia has become a party to the conflict by virtue of its commitment of troops to fight in Azerbaijan against the Azerbaijani armed forces. Armenia also gives substantial assistance to the rebels.

The rules of war are based on an artificial distinction between international armed conflicts and non-international (internal) armed conflicts, with different rules for each. Thus a different legal scheme applies to the parties according to their legal character (whether they are states or rebels) and to the conventions to which the state parties have acceded.

The original conflict, between Azerbaijan and its citizens of Armenian origin in the enclave of Nagorno-Karabakh (with support from Armenians living in the then Armenian SSR), is an internal armed conflict governed by the provisions of Article 3 common to the four Geneva Conventions of 1949.[323] Common Article 3 expressly binds all parties to the internal conflict, including insurgents such as the militia of Nagorno-Karabakh, although they do not have the legal capacity to sign the Geneva

---

[322]*See* Hans-Peter Gasser, "Internationalized Non-International Armed Conflicts: Case Studies of Afghanistan, Kampuchea, and Lebanon." *American University Law Review* 33 (Washington, D.C.: 1983): pp. 145 *et seq*.

[323]Article 3 common to the four Geneva Conventions of 1949, section 1, applies "[i]n the case of an armed conflict not of an international character occurring in the territory of one of the High Contracting Parties . . . ." Azerbaijan is a High Contracting Party to the four Geneva Convention as of June 1, 1993. Protocol II of 1977 to the 1949 Geneva Conventions is a principal source of rules governing the conduct of hostilities in internal armed conflicts. Although Azerbaijan has not acceded to Protocol II, this Protocol nevertheless contains rules that provide authoritative guidance to both the government and the rebels for the protection of the civilian population in this internal conflict.

Conventions.[324]

Application of common Article 3 cannot be construed as recognition of the independence or belligerence of the Nagorno-Karabakh rebels, from which recognition of additional legal obligations would flow. Nor is it necessary for any government to recognize the independence or belligerent status of these rebels for common Article 3 to apply.

As to the conflict between the Republic of Armenia and the Republic of Azerbaijan, common Article 2 to the four Geneva Conventions of 1949 states that the Conventions "shall apply to all cases of declared war or of any other armed conflict which may arise between two or more of the High Contracting Parties, even if the state of war is not recognized by one of them."[325]

All that is required to trigger the definition of international armed conflict is the occurrence of *de facto* hostilities between Armenia and Azerbaijan, which is defined as use of members of the armed forces.

> Any difference arising between two States and leading to the intervention of members of the armed forces is an armed conflict within the meaning of Article 2, even if one of the Parties denies the existence of a state of war. It makes no difference how long the conflict lasts, or how much slaughter takes place. The respect due to the human person is not measured by the number of victims.[326]

Armenia has used its armed forces to conduct hostilities on Azerbaijani territory against members of the Azerbaijani armed forces, which have attacked those Armenian forces in turn.

In addition, soldiers of both states have engaged in cross-border shelling, especially in the Qazakh, Agstafa, and Tovuz area of Azerbaijan and in the Noyembrian, Ijevan, and Tavush regions of Armenia. The two republics both hold as prisoners of war soldiers from each other's army. In addition, the Azerbaijani enclaves of Kyarki, Yukhari Askipara, and Barkhudarly inside Armenia have been occupied by the Armenian army and the Azeris who lived there expelled to Azerbaijan proper.

---

[324]As private individuals within the national territory of a State Party, certain obligations are imposed on insurgents. International Committee of the Red Cross, *Commentary on the Additional Protocols of 1977* (Geneva: International Committee of the Red Cross, 1987), p. 1345.

[325]Armenia acceded to the conventions on June 7, 1993, thereby becoming a High Contracting Party. Armenia acceded to Protocols I and II of 1977 to the Geneva Conventions on the same date.

[326]International Committee of the Red Cross, *Commentary on IV Geneva Convention* (Geneva: International Committee of the Red Cross, 1958), p. 20-21.

Likewise, the Armenian enclave of Artsvashen inside Azerbaijan was seized by the Azerbaijani army and the Armenians expelled.

The Republic of Armenia has claimed that all Armenian citizens participating in hostilities in Nagorno-Karabakh or Azerbaijan are merely "volunteers." Human Rights Watch/Helsinki found that this claim is not true. While there are probably volunteers to the rebel forces from among the Republic of Armenia population, active duty members of the Armenian armed forces, including conscripts, have been ordered by their military commanders to participate in hostilities in Azerbaijan against the Azerbaijani armed forces. Some Republic of Armenian soldiers have died in battle in Azerbaijan and have been buried in the Republic of Armenia military cemetery with full military honors. It is reported that the widows of Armenian citizens killed fighting in Nagorno-Karabakh receive state support.

Armenia holds in its prisons some Azerbaijani soldiers captured in combat as well as Azerbaijani civilians captured in Armenian-occupied areas of Azerbaijan. They are exchanged for Armenian prisoners of war and civilians held by Azerbaijani authorities.

In addition to committing troops to the conflict against Azerbaijan and in support of the Nagorno-Karabakh rebels, the Republic of Armenia also has provided material aid to the rebels, although this is not necessary to make the conflict an international one. By the admission of Karabakh officials, Armenia supplies as much as 90 percent of the enclave's budget in the form of interest-free credits; these payments may total between 7-9 percent of Armenia's total budget. Armenian troops and other aid have helped the Nagorno-Karabakh rebels, a force of some 30,000 drawn from a total Nagorno-Karabakh population of Armenian origin of only about 145,000, to occupy not only the mountainous Nagorno-Karabakh enclave (10 percent of Azerbaijan's total territory) but also occupy another 10 percent of Azerbaijani territory surrounding Karabakh on the east, south, and west, and to expel all Azeris resident in these territories, over 500,000 people.

Common Article 2 states that the 1949 Geneva Conventions "shall also apply to all cases of partial or total occupation of the territory of a High Contracting Party, even if the said occupation meets with no armed resistance." Approximately 20 percent of the territory of Azerbaijan has been occupied by the Nagorno-Karabakh rebels, at times with the support of Republic of Armenia troops.

The conduct of the Republic of Armenia is governed by Protocol I as well, applicable also to international armed conflicts. Since the Republic of Azerbaijan has not acceded to Protocol I, its conduct is not governed by Protocol I. Many of the relevant provisions of Protocol I, however, are reflective of customary international humanitarian law, which applies to all parties to the conflict.

The obligation to apply these humanitarian law provisions is absolute for all parties to the conflict and independent of the obligation of the other parties. That means that one party cannot excuse itself from complying with the rules of war applicable to it on the grounds that another party is violating them, and vice versa.

CUSTOMARY INTERNATIONAL LAW APPLICABLE TO
INTERNATIONAL ARMED CONFLICTS

Prisoners of War

One principle difference between the rules applicable to internal and international armed conflicts is the treatment of captured combatants. The combatant's privilege[327] applies in international armed conflicts, but not in internal armed conflicts.

Captured combatants in international armed conflicts are prisoners of war. The minimum treatment they must receive is detailed in the Third Geneva Convention.

Prisoners of war include members of the armed forces of a party to the conflict as well as members of militia or volunteer corps forming part of such armed forces, who have "fallen into the power of the enemy."[328] Thus the members of the Republic of Armenia armed forces who have been captured by Azerbaijani government forces are prisoners of war, and indeed the Azerbaijani government refers to them as such.

Members of the Azerbaijani armed forces captured by the Armenian armed forces are also prisoners of war. Unless the Republic of Armenia then holds them or otherwise is involved in their detention, those who are captured solely by the rebels probably do not qualify as prisoner of war under the Third Geneva Convention. It appears that the rebels do treat the captured Azerbaijani forces as prisoners of war.

Nagorno-Karabakh rebels do not enjoy any special status when captured.[329] The Azerbaijani government is not obliged to grant captured Nagorno-Karabakh rebels prisoner of war status. It may, however, agree to treat its rebel captives as prisoners of war, and appears to have done so.[330]

The term "prisoners of war" is restricted to captured combatants and does not

---

[327]The combatant's privilege is a license to kill or capture enemy troops, destroy military objectives and cause unavoidable civilian casualties. This privilege immunizes members of armed forces or rebels from criminal prosecution by their captors for their violent acts that do not violate the laws of war but would otherwise be crimes under domestic law. Prisoner of war status depends on and flows from this privilege. *See* Solf, "The Status of Combatants in Non-International Armed Conflicts Under Domestic Law and Transnational Practice," *American University Law Review* 33 (Washington, D.C.: 1953): p. 59.

[328]III Geneva, Art. 4 (A)(1).

[329]Since the rebels are not privileged combatants as a matter of law, they may be tried and punished by the Azerbaijani government for murder, destruction of property, and the commission of other crimes under Azerbaijani domestic law.

[330]The Azerbaijani *de facto* recognition of captured Karabakh rebels as prisoners of war precludes the need to examine whether the rebels are militia belonging to a party to the conflict, *i.e.*, Republic of Armenia. III Geneva, Art. 4 (A)(2).

include civilians.

Mistreatment of Prisoners of War

Willful killing, torture or inhuman treatment, and willfully causing great suffering or serious injury to body or health, of a prisoner of war are grave breaches of the Geneva Conventions. Willfully depriving a prisoner of war of the rights of fair and regular trial prescribed in the Third Geneva Convention is also a grave breach.[331] Prisoners of war need not be tried at all; because of the combatants' privilege, they may not be tried for military activities that do not violate the rules of war.

Civilians in Occupied Territory

Civilians residing in territory occupied by a party to the international conflict, in this case Azerbaijani civilians residing in Azerbaijani territory occupied by the Republic of Armenia armed forces, are entitled to extensive protection detailed in the Fourth Geneva Convention.

Corporal punishment, torture, murder and brutality toward "protected persons" is forbidden.[332] Civilians in occupied territories who have been detained or interned[333] have rights comparable to those of prisoners of war and may not be compelled to work.

Furthermore, labor by the undetained civilians in occupied territories is regulated. Such labor may be compelled for the needs of the occupying army only, and the work must be performed only in occupied territory. It must be in keeping with the physical capabilities of the worker and must be compensated at a fair wage.[334]

LAW APPLICABLE IN INTERNAL CONFLICTS

Common Article 3 is a convention within a convention. It provides:

> In the case of armed conflict not of an international character occurring in the territory of one of the High Contracting Parties, each Party to the conflict shall be bound to apply, as a minimum, the following provisions:
> (I)   Persons taking no active part in the hostilities, including

---

[331]III Geneva, Art. 130.

[332]IV Geneva, Art. 32. "Protected persons "are those who find themselves in the hands of a party to the conflict or occupying power of which they are not nationals. IV Geneva, Art. 4.

[333]IV Geneva, Art. 76 *et seq* (detainee) and 79 (internees).

[334]IV Geneva, Art. 51.

members of armed forces who have laid down their arms and those placed *hors de combat* by sickness, wounds, detention, or any other cause, shall in all circumstances be treated humanely, without any adverse distinction founded on race, color, religion or faith, sex, birth or wealth, or any other similar criteria.

To this end, the following acts are and shall remain prohibited at any time and in any place whatsoever with respect to the above-mentioned persons:

(a) violence to life and person, in particular murder of all kinds, mutilation, cruel treatment and torture;

(b) taking of hostages;

(c) outrages upon personal dignity, in particular humiliating and degrading treatment;

(d) the passing of sentences and the carrying out of executions without previous judgment pronounced by a regularly constituted court, affording all the judicial guarantees which are recognized as indispensable by civilized peoples.

(2) The wounded and sick shall be collected and cared for. Customary international humanitarian law in addition to common Article 3 applies to all countries.[335]

CUSTOMARY INTERNATIONAL LAW APPLICABLE TO BOTH INTERNAL AND INTERNATIONAL ARMED CONFLICTS

Attacks against the civilian population are prohibited by the customary laws of armed conflict. United Nations General Assembly Resolution 2444, adopted by unanimous vote on December 19, 1969, expressly recognized the customary law principle of civilian immunity and its complementary principle requiring the warring parties to distinguish civilians from combatants at all times. The preamble to this resolution clearly states that these fundamental humanitarian law principles apply "in all armed conflicts," meaning both international and internal armed conflicts. United Nations Resolution 2444 affirms:

. . . the following principles for observance by all government and other authorities responsible for action in armed conflicts:

(a) That the right of the parties to a conflict to adopt

---

[335]*See, e.g.,* Theodor Meron, *Human Rights and Humanitarian Norms and Customary Law* (Oxford: Clarendon Press, 1989).

means of injuring the enemy is not unlimited;

(b) That it is prohibited to launch attacks against the civilian populations as such;

(c) That distinction must be made at all times between persons taking part in the hostilities and members of the civilian population to the effect that the latter be spared as much as possible.[336]

Protection of the Civilian Population during Conflict

In situations of armed conflict, generally speaking, a civilian is anyone who is not a member of the armed forces or of an organized armed group of a party to the conflict. Accordingly, "the civilian population comprises all persons who do not actively participate in the hostilities."[337]

Civilians may not be subject to deliberate individualized attack since they pose no immediate threat to the adversary.[338]

The term "civilian" also includes some employees of the military establishment who are not members of the armed forces or militia but assist them. While as civilians they may not be targeted, these civilian employees of military establishments or those who indirectly assist combatants assume the risk of death or injury incidental to attacks against legitimate military targets while they are at or in the immediate vicinity of military targets.

In addition, both sides utilize as part-time combatants persons who are otherwise engaged in civilian occupations. These civilians lose their immunity from attack for as long as they directly participate in hostilities.[339] "[D]irect participation [in hostilities] means acts of war which by their nature and purpose are likely to cause actual harm to the personnel and equipment of enemy armed forces," and includes acts of defense.[340]

"Hostilities" not only covers the time when the civilian actually makes use of a weapon but also the time that he is carrying it, as well as situations in which he

---

[336]*Respect for Human Rights in Armed Conflicts*, United Nations Resolution 2444, G.A. Res. 2444, 23 U.N. GAOR Supp. (No. 18) at 164, U.N. Doc. A/7433 (1968).

[337]R. Goldman, "International Humanitarian Law and the Armed Conflicts in El Salvador and Nicaragua," *American University Journal of International Law & Policy* 2 (1987), p. 553.

[338]M. Bothe, K. Partsch, & W. Solf, *New Rules for Victims of Armed Conflicts: Commentary on the Two 1977 Protocols Additional to the Geneva Conventions of 1949* (Geneva: Martins Nijhoff, 1982), p.303.

[339]*Ibid.*

[340]ICRC, *Commentary on the Two 1977 Protocols*, p. 619.

undertakes hostile acts without using a weapon.[341] Examples are provided in the United States Army Field Manual which lists some hostile acts

> as including sabotage, destruction of communication facilities, intentional misleading of troops by guides, and liberation of prisoners of war. . . . This is also the case of a person acting as a member of a weapons crew, or one providing target information for weapon systems intended for immediate use against the enemy such as artillery spotters or members of ground observer teams. [It] would include direct logistic support for units engaged directly in battle such as the delivery of ammunition to a firing position. On the other hand civilians providing only indirect support to the armed forces, such as workers in defense plants or those engaged in distribution or storage of military supplies in rear areas, do not pose an immediate threat to the adversary and therefore would not be subject to deliberate individual attack.[342]

Once their participation in hostilities ceases, that is, while engaged in their civilian vocations, these civilians may not be attacked.

Persons protected by customary law include members of the government or rebel armed forces who surrender, are wounded, sick or unarmed, or are captured. They are *hors de combat*, literally, out of combat, until such time as they take a hostile action such as attempting to escape.

Detainees

While they are in the power of a party to the conflict, combatants as well as civilians are protected against violence to life and person, including among other things murder, cruel treatment, torture, attacks on personal dignity and summary execution.[343]

Designation of Military Objectives

To constitute a legitimate military objective, the object or target must contribute effectively to the enemy's military capability or activity, and its destruction must offer a definite military advantage. The definition has been codified in Protocol I:

---

[341]*Ibid.*, pp. 618-619. This is a broader definition than "attacks" and includes at a minimum preparation for combat and return from combat. Bothe, *New Rules for Victims of Armed Conflicts*, p. 303.

[342]Quoted in Bothe, *New Rules for Victims of Armed Conflicts*, p. 303 (footnote omitted).

[343]Article 3 common to the four Geneva Conventions of 1949.

1. Civilian objects shall not be the object of attack or of reprisals. Civilian objects are all objects which are not military objects as defined in paragraph 2.

2. Attacks shall be limited strictly to military objectives. In so far as objects are concerned, military objectives are limited to those objects which by their nature, location, purpose or use make an effective contribution to military action and whose total or partial destruction, capture or neutralization, in the circumstances ruling at the time, offers a definite military advantage.[344]

Members of the armed forces and rebels are legitimate military targets and subject to attack, individually or collectively, until such time as they become *hors de combat*, that is, surrender or are wounded or captured.[345]

Whatever their original occupation, the Karabakh paramilitaries we interviewed were combatants, armed and operating under a command structure. Many are engaged full-time in military duties, defense as well as offense.

Even when not participating full-time in hostilities, paramilitaries like other civilians lose their immunity from attack whenever they assume a combatant's role. Thus, when they prepare for, actively participate in and return from combat (while carrying a weapon or committing hostile acts without using a weapon), they are proper military targets.

Other legitimate military objectives are combatants' weapons, convoys, installations, and supplies. In addition,

an object generally used for civilian purposes, such as a dwelling, a bus, a fleet of taxicabs, or a civilian airfield or railroad siding, can become a military objective if its location or use meets both of the criteria set forth. . . .[346]

Policemen without combat duties are not legitimate military targets. The drafters of the protocols intended to exclude from the definition of "armed forces" policemen as well as other government personnel authorized to bear arms such as customs agents. Policemen with combat duties, however, would be proper military targets, subject to direct individualized attack.

---

[344]Protocol I, Art. 52 (2). This codifies customary international law.

[345]This explains why killing a wounded or captured combatant is not proper: it does not offer a "definite military advantage in the circumstances" because the fighter is already rendered useless or *hors de combat*.

[346]Bothe, referred to *New Rules for Victims of Armed Conflict*, pp. 306-07. The criteria are those defining military objectives in Protocol I, Art. 52 (2).

Civilian Objects

The laws of war implicitly characterize all objects as civilian unless they satisfy the two-fold test of military objective. Objects normally dedicated to civilian use, such as churches, houses and schools, are presumed not to be military objectives. If they in fact do assist the enemy's military action, they can lose their immunity from direct attack. This presumption attaches, however, only to objects that ordinarily have no significant military use or purpose. For example, this presumption would not include objects such as transportation and communications systems that under applicable criteria are military objectives.

For purposes of this conflict, the following should be considered civilian objects immune from direct attack by combatants:

— Structures and locales, such as houses, churches, mosques, dwellings, schools, and farm villages, that are exclusively dedicated to civilian purposes and, in the circumstances prevailing at the time, do not make an effective contribution to military action.

Legitimate Military Targets

While not an exhaustive list, the following persons, groups, and objects may be regarded as legitimate military objectives subject to direct attack:

— Rebels both full time and part-time, while the latter are directly participating in hostilities.

— Members of the police, while they have combat duties.

— Members of paramilitary groups as long as they are directly participating in hostilities.

— Weapons, other war material, military works, military and naval establishments, supplies, vehicles, campsites, fortifications, and fuel depots or stores that are utilized by any party to the conflict.

— Objects that, while not directly connected with combat operations, effectively contribute to military operations, and whose partial or total capture, destruction, or neutralization, in the circumstances ruling at the time, would result in a definite and concrete military advantage to the attacker.

Destruction and Pillage of Civilian Objects

Pillage, which encompasses looting or taking as booty or spoils of war, is forbidden by the Fourth Geneva Convention[347] as well as by customary law. This prohibition covers individual acts without the consent of the military authorities and also organized pillage. The ordering or authorization is forbidden, and the parties are obliged to prevent or, if it has commenced, to stop individual pillage. All types of property, whether private, communal, or state, are protected, although the military authorities retain the right to requisition goods under the conditions set forth in Article 55 of the Fourth Geneva Convention.[348] The purpose of this old principle of humanitarian law is to spare people the suffering resulting from the destruction of their real and personal property.[349]

Destruction of property not absolutely necessary on account of military operations also is forbidden by the Fourth Geneva Convention[350] and by customary law.[351] All types of property in occupied territory are protected from destruction except where such destruction is rendered absolutely necessary by military operations. When done unlawfully and wantonly such destruction is a grave breach of the Geneva Conventions.[352]

Prohibition of Indiscriminate Attacks Affecting Civilians and Civilian Objects; the Principle of Proportionality

The civilian population and individual civilians are protected against direct attack.[353] The rules in Protocol I that protect civilians from such attacks provide relevant guidance for interpreting the extent of this protection. Article 51(4) of Protocol I, for instance, expressly protects the civilian population from indiscriminate or disproportionate attacks.[354]

As set forth above, to constitute a legitimate military object, the target must 1) contribute effectively to the enemy's military capability or activity, and 2) its total or partial destruction or neutralization must offer a definite military advantage in the

---

[347]IV Geneva, Art. 33.

[348]ICRC, *Commentary on the IV Geneva Convention*, pp. 226-27.

[349]*Ibid.*, p. 226.

[350]IV Geneva, Art. 53.

[351]Meron, *Human Rights and Humanitarian Norms as Customary Law*, pp. 46-47.

[352]IV Geneva, Art. 147.

[353]U.N. Resolution 2444.

[354]The article prohibits attacks that are not directed at specific military objectives or that employ a method or means of combat that a party cannot direct at a specific military objective.

circumstances.

Even attacks on legitimate military targets are limited by the principle of proportionality. This principle places a duty on combatants to choose means of attack that avoid or minimize damage to civilians. In particular, the attacker should refrain from launching an attack if the expected civilian casualties would outweigh the importance of the military target to the attacker. For example, an attack on an entire town or village in order to destroy a number of clearly separate military targets that could be attacked separately would be indiscriminate. But attacks carefully directed against each military target within that location, using accurate means of attack, would not be indiscriminate.

The attacker also must do everything "feasible" to verify that the objectives to be attacked are not civilians. "Feasible" means "that which is practical or practically possible taking into account all the circumstances at the time, including those relevant to the success of military operations."[355]

The means used to attack legitimate military targets must be carefully chosen and all feasible precautions taken in their choice with a view to avoiding, and in any event to minimizing, incidental loss of civilian life, injury to civilians, and damage to civilian objects. Effective advance warning must be given of attacks that might affect the civilian population, unless circumstances do not permit.[356]

Starvation of Civilians as a Method of Warfare[357]

Starvation of civilians as a method of warfare has become illegal as a matter of customary law, as reflected in Protocol I, Article 54 (1) - (2):[358]

> 1. Starvation of civilians as a method of warfare is prohibited.
> 2. It is prohibited to attack, destroy, remove or render useless objects indispensable to the survival of the civilian population,

---

[355]Bothe. *New Rules for Victims of Armed Conflict.* p. 362.

[356]*See* Protocol I, Article 57.

[357]None of the blockades or embargoes in this conflict meet the criteria of starvation of civilians as a method of warfare or combat set forth in international law.

[358]Protocol II, Article 14, contains a similar prohibition:

Article 14 —— Protection of objects indispensable to the survival of the civilian population

> Starvation of civilians as a method of combat is prohibited. It is prohibited to attack, destroy, remove or render useless, for that purpose, objects indispensable to the survival of the civilian population, such as foodstuffs, agricultural areas for the production of foodstuffs, crops, livestock, drinking water installations and supplies and irrigation works.

such as foodstuffs, agricultural areas for the production of foodstuffs, crops, livestock, drinking water installations and supplies and irrigation works, for the specific purpose of denying them for their sustenance value to the civilian population or to the adverse Party, whatever the motive, whether in order to starve out civilians, to cause them to move away, or for any other motive.

What is prohibited is using starvation as "a weapon to annihilate or weaken the population."[359] Using starvation as a method of warfare or combat does not mean that the population has to reach the point of starving to death before a violation can be proved. What is forbidden is deliberately "causing the population to suffer hunger, particularly by depriving it of its sources of food or of supplies."[360]

This prohibition on starving civilians "is a rule from which no derogation may be made."[361] No exception was made for imperative military necessity, for instance.

Article 54 lists the most usual ways in which starvation is brought about. Specific protection is extended to "objects indispensable to the survival of the civilian population," and a non-exhaustive list of such objects follows: "foodstuffs, agricultural areas for the production of foodstuffs, crops, livestock, drinking water installations and supplies and irrigation works." The article prohibits taking certain destructive actions aimed at these essential supplies, and describes these actions with verbs which are meant to cover all eventualities: "attack, destroy, remove or render useless."

The textual reference to "objects indispensable to the survival of the civilian population"

does not distinguish between objects intended for the armed forces and those intended for civilians. Except for the case where supplies are specifically intended as provisions for combatants, it is prohibited to destroy or attack objects indispensable for survival, even if the adversary may benefit from them. The prohibition would be meaningless if one could invoke the argument that members of the government's armed forces or armed opposition might make use of the objects in question.[362]

---

[359]ICRC. *Commentary on The Additional Protocols.* p. 653.

[360]*Ibid.*

[361]*Ibid.,* p. 1456.

[362]*Ibid.,* pp. 1458-59.

Attacks on objects used "in direct support of military action" are permissible, however, even if these objects are civilian foodstuffs and other objects protected under Article 54. This exception is limited to the immediate zone of actual armed engagements, as is obvious from the examples provided of military objects used in direct support of military action: "bombarding a food-producing area to prevent the army from advancing through it, or attacking a food storage barn which is being used by the enemy for cover or as an arms depot, etc."[363]

It is permitted, however, to attack military food supplies under Article 54 (3). It specifically limits such attacks to those directed at foodstuffs intended for the sole use of the enemy's armed forces. This means "supplies already in the hands of the adverse party's armed forces because it is only at that point that one could know that they are intended for use only for the members of the enemy's armed forces."[364] Even then, the attacker cannot destroy foodstuffs "in the military supply system intended for the sustenance of prisoners of war, the civilian population of occupied territory or persons classified as civilians serving with, or accompanying, the armed forces."[365]

Proof of Intention to Starve Civilians

Under Article 54, what is forbidden are actions taken with the intention of using starvation as a method or weapon to attack the civilian population. Such an intention may not be easy to prove and most armies will not admit this intention. Proof does not rest solely on the attacker's own statements, however. Intention may be inferred from the totality of the circumstances of the military campaign.

Particularly relevant to assessment of intention is the effort the attacker makes to comply with the duties to distinguish between civilians and military targets and to avoid harming civilians and the civilian economy.[366] If the attacker does not comply with these duties, and food shortages result, an intention to attack civilians by starvation may be inferred.

The more sweeping and indiscriminate the measures taken which result in food shortages, when other less restrictive means of combat are available, the more

---

[363]*Ibid.*, p. 657. The *New Rules* gives the following examples of direct support: "an irrigation canal used as part of a defensive position, a water tower used as an observation post, or a cornfield used as cover for the infiltration of an attacking force." Bothe, *New Rules for Victims of Armed Conflicts*, p. 341.

[364]Bothe, *New Rules for Victims of Armed Conflict*, p. 340.

[365]*Ibid.*, pp. 340-41.

[366]Civilians are not legitimate military targets; this is expressly forbidden by U.N. General Assembly Resolution 2444, above. The duty to distinguish at all times between civilians and combatants, and between civilian objects and military objects, includes the duty to direct military operations only against military objectives.

likely the real intention is to attack the civilian population by causing it food deprivation. For instance, an attacker who conducts a scorched earth campaign in enemy territory to deprive the enemy of sources of food may be deemed to have an intention of attacking by starvation the civilian population living in enemy territory. The attacker may not claim ignorance of the effects upon civilians of such a scorched earth campaign, since these effects are a matter of common knowledge and publicity. In particular, relief organizations, both domestic and international, usually sound the alarm of impending food shortages occurring during conflicts in order to bring pressure on the parties to permit access for food delivery and to raise money for their complex and costly operations.

The true intentions of the attacker also must be judged by the effort it makes to take prompt remedies, such as permitting relief convoys to reach the needy or itself supplying food to remedy hunger. An attacker who fails to make adequate provision for the affected civilian population, who blocks access to those who would do so, or who refuses to permit civilian evacuation in times of food shortage, may be deemed to have the intention to starve that civilian population.

APPENDIX B. POINTS OF VIEW

REPUBLIC OF AZERBAIJAN

Azeris view themselves as the aggrieved party in the conflict, their territorial integrity violated and land occupied. They consider Karabakh historically Azeri and point to large-scale Armenian migration to the region after Russian conquest of the areas comprising present-day Armenia and Azerbaijan in 1813 and 1828. They deny that Armenians in Karabakh during the Soviet period suffered discrimination, claiming that most economic indicators were higher in Nagorno-Karabakh than in the rest of Azerbaijan. Most Azeris believe that the Gorbachev government was hopelessly pro-Armenian because of his Armenian advisers, and that world opinion blindly supports Armenia and Armenians, viewing them as "eternal victims" even though more than 20 percent of Azerbaijan is occupied by Armenian forces and approximately one million Azeris are internally displaced or refugees. Vagif Sadykhov, chief of the Political-Military Section of the Azerbaijani Foreign Ministry complained that, "No NGOs or international organizations are giving an objective judgement of the situation. . . applying the same standards and demanding both observe the same standards. They do not see the differences. Azerbaijan is trying to protect and restore its sovereignty."[367]

The Azerbaijani government insists it remains committed to a peaceful settlement of the conflict, but is completely opposed to changing radically the present status of Nagorno-Karabakh. The Azerbaijani government has mostly refused to meet bilaterally with representatives of the self-proclaimed Republic of Nagorno-Karabakh, often viewing the Republic of Armenia as its main negotiating partner. It also demands the withdrawal of Armenian forces from occupied Azerbaijani territory as a basic precondition for negotiations. Azerbaijani President Aliyev stated that,

> I suggested to Moscow and to Levon Ter-Petrosyan, 'Look, let's withdraw these troops from the occupied territory of Azerbaijan with the exception of Nagorno-Karabakh. And then we will really have negotiations about Karabakh.' This could have been a point of contact the Armenians really could have utilized, but they said: 'considering our military superiority and plus the fact that we occupy your territory, grant Karabakh independence.' This of course is unacceptable.[368]

---

[367]Interview, Baku, Azerbaijan, March 24, 1994.

[368]Russian Television, "Labirint — Karabakhskaya Drama: Put' K Soglasiyu," May 7, 1994.

If Armenian troops are withdrawn, the Azerbaijanis say, a discussion on the status of Karabakh is possible. Vafa Goulizade, a State Counsellor to the President of Azerbaijan, said "The Armenians can have full cultural and economic rights, plus a humanitarian corridor under international supervision, but not independence."[369] President Aliyev stated that "We have affirmed and continue to affirm that the security and rights of the Armenian population of Nagorno-Karabakh are guaranteed by the Azerbaijani Constitution and by state organs. If a resolution is passed about the unconditional withdrawal of Armenian forces from the occupied territories, then the Azerbaijani side can examine the question about the status of Nagorno-Karabakh."[370]

Azerbaijan sees the hand of Armenia and Russia in the conflict. Armenia is said to be motivated by a desire for territorial expansion, and Russia by the desire to punish Azerbaijan for too much independence: belatedly joining the CIS and not permitting Russian troops to be based in Azerbaijan. Azerbaijan has for the most part refused to deal directly in negotiations with the Karabakh Armenians. Claiming that the war is run from the Armenian Defense Ministry in Yerevan, they point to soldiers captured in Azerbaijan from the Army of the Republic of Armenia, military equipment from Armenian army stocks, and maps and orders from the Armenian Defense Ministry seized on the battlefield. They note the August 1993 appointment of the Karabakh Defense Minister Serzhik Sarkissian as the Defense Minister of the Republic of Armenia.[371] They protest that, "the Armenian population in Nagorno-Karabakh had autonomy. . . . The conflict did not arise because they did not have autonomy, but because certain circles in Armenia and Nagorno-Karabakh tried to unite Karabakh and Armenia."[372] Azeris also believe that the December 1, 1989 Armenian Supreme Soviet decision, "Reunification of the Armenian SSR and Nagorny Karabakh" clearly shows Armenian intent to seize and annex Azerbaijani territory.[373] In Azerbaijan one often hears about Armenian plans for a "Greater Armenia."

---

[369]Interview, Baku, Azerbaijan, March 25, 1994.

[370]"Press Konferentsiya," *Bakinskii Rabochii,* Baku, March 25, 1994.

[371]The Permanent Mission of the Republic of Azerbaijan introduced evidence concerning Armenian military involvement
in the conflict to the United Nations in early 1994. See United Nations Security Council Documents S/1994/141-2-9-94 and S/1994/108-2-2-94.

[372]President Aliyev on a visit to China in March 1994. "Press-Konferentsiya Prezidenta Azerbaidzhana Geidara Aliyeva v Pekine," *Bakinskii Rabochii,* Baku, March 25, 1994.

[373]United Nations Security Council, "Letter dated 10 February 1994 from the Charge D'Affaires A.I. of the Permanent Mission of Azerbaijan to the United Nations Addressed to the Secretary General."

Azeris also are extremely suspicious of Russian intentions and view their support of Armenia as a rather crude way of pressuring Azerbaijan and its oil wealth back into Moscow's economic and security sphere of influence. Russian defense officials would especially like to base troops on the sensitive Azerbaijani-Iranian border; the last Russian troops left Azerbaijan in May 1993. While Armenia willingly joined CIS and welcomed Russian troops and bases on its territory, Azerbaijan only joined CIS after the fiercely anti-Moscow president, Abulfaz Elchibey, was ousted in a June 1993 coup that brought to power the former USSR Politburo member and Azerbaijani Communist Party First Party Secretary Heidar Aliyev. Even he continues to resist the entry of Russian military forces on Azerbaijani territory.[374] Azerbaijan opposes the deployment of a Russian-only peacekeeping force during a cease-fire and seeks an international presence, a demand that seems to be satisfied under the OSCE's December 1994 decision to send a multinational force.

One high-ranking Azerbaijani Foreign Ministry official commented, "The Armenians themselves told us that the Russians wanted them to occupy Kelbajar. Russia wants to base troops here again, it's quite obvious. We're told in negotiations: 'Let Russian troops come to Azerbaijan, and you will have peace.'[375] The Azerbaijani President Aliyev noted that, "there are Russian troops based in Armenia. They have the status of military bases. This is not the case in Azerbaijan. This very fact has great meaning to any right-minded individual in light of the war that is going on between Azerbaijan and Armenia."[376]

Azeris suspect Russia is intent on cashing in on Azerbaijan's oil wealth, pointing to Moscow's initiative to redefine the status of the Caspian Sea and its interference in plans to build a pipeline to carry Azeri oil to the west.[377] After

---

[374]From a strategic point of view, Armenia wanted Russian troops to patrol its western border with Turkey. Most Armenians with whom Human Rights Watch/Helsinki spoke saw little danger of Russian influence because of Armenians' well-developed national feeling.

Azerbaijan, on the other hand, in May 1993, was the first CIS country to achieve the complete withdrawal of Russian troops.

[375]Interview, March 1994, Baku, Azerbaijan. Vladimir Kazimirov is the Russian envoy assigned to the Karabakh conflict.

[376]"Karabakhskaya Drama," *op. cit.*

[377]During the Soviet period and presently, the Caspian Sea had the status of a lake, meaning that it was equally divided into sections among littoral states. Under this formula, many of the best offshore oil fields fell to Azerbaijan. Were the Caspian to receive the status of a sea or ocean, littoral states would only have rights twelve miles from their shore; the rest would be international waters, subject to negotiation concerning mineral resources. Most of Azerbaijan's offshore oil fields are located more than twelve miles from Azerbaijan's coast.

Azerbaijan — and most Western oil companies — prefer a direct pipeline from Azeri

Azerbaijan signed a $7 billion dollar oil deal to develop three oil fields with a Western consortium on September 20, 1994, Russia immediately raised demands for redefining the status of the Caspian Sea: Russian Foreign Ministry spokesman Grigory Karasin stated that Russia would not "officially" recognize the deal, adding that, "Unilateral actions, especially on resources and the Caspian Sea, contradict international law.. ."[378]

NAGORNO-KARABAKH ARMENIANS

Karabakh Armenians characterize their struggle as an ancient one of self-determination against an outside, repressive power. To them, Karabakh — or Artsakh as they refer to it — is an ancient cultural and religious center of Armenians. Robert Kocharian, the Chairman of the Karabakh Defense Committee, commented that, "Nations that live somewhere always leave traces, churches, monuments. I think it is enough to walk the Karabakh territory to see who has lived there and left traces."[379] The Karabakh Armenians view their sixty-odd years of cohabitation with Azeris in the Azerbaijani Soviet Socialist Republic as a time of cultural repression and economic underdevelopment.

The Karabakh Armenians believe that the independence referendum they held in December 1991 fully justifies their January 6, 1992 declaration of independence. In an interview this year with the Armenian-American magazine *AIM*, Nagorno-Karabakh Foreign Minister Arkadii Gukasyan stated that, "Our referendum voted for the independence of Nagorno-Karabakh. We proceed from that basic point. Our position today is the following: Nagorno-Karabakh should have its own status of sovereignty." Consequently, the Karabakh Armenians believe that Azerbaijan should negotiate directly with them, not with the Republic of Armenia, to bring an end to the conflict.[380] To date no state — including Armenia — has recognized this sovereignty. In May 1994, State Defense Committee head Kocharian — elected as President by Parliament in December 1994 — affirmed the goal of independence from

---

oil fields to Turkey on the Mediterranean. Russia, on the other hand, wants a pipeline that goes through its territory and exits at Novorossisk on the Black Sea.

[378]Brian Killen, "Azerbaijan, Western Firms sign Caspian Deal," Reuters, September 20, 1994.

[379]*Yerkir* (Yerevan, Armenia), January 12, 1994. Often a visitor to Karabakh will receive as a gift H. H. Hakopyan's *The Medival Art of Artsakh*.

[380]Nagorno-Karabakh Foreign Minister Arkady Gukasyan commented that. "Today Karabakh is de facto independent. . . . I don't see any alternative to direct talks between both sides. *Nagorno-Karabakh*, April 1994, #1.

Azerbaijan.[381] Mr. Melik Shakhnazaryan, the Chairman of the Foreign Affairs Committee of the Karabakh parliament, told Human Rights Watch/Helsinki that his people's ultimate goal remained complete independence.[382]

The Karabakh Armenians insist that security, a concern motivating their 1993 seizure of all Azerbaijani territory surrounding Nagorno-Karabakh, represents a key issue in bringing a resolution to the conflict. Such considerations lay behind Karabakh's capture of Kelbajar and the rest of the Azerbaijani territory it seized in 1993: to create a "safe rear area and to prevent shelling." According to the Chairman of Nagorno-Karabakh's Defense Committee, Robert Kocharian, "[In order] to answer the large-scale March 1993 offensive against the Mardakert region and the Lachin Corridor by the Azerbaijani Army [coming from Kelbajar province], NKR authorities were forced to order our army to destroy the enemy's strong points ['opornyye punkty'] representing the greatest threat to Nagorno-Karabakh."[383] They seized all NKAO areas to prevent bombardments from Azerbaijani forces into their territory, they claim. While the Karabakh Armenians state that they remain committed to all peace initiatives, they must not come at the expense of the safety of Karabakh's population. In an interview with the American-Armenian publication *AIM*, Kocharian stated that, "We should be completely be assured that the territory returned will not be used as a base to commence military action." Consequently a "land for peace status" relationship has formed.

The Karabakh Armenians repeatedly claim they do not intend to hold most of the territory they captured outside of the borders of Nagorno-Karabakh.[384]

---

[381]He stated that,"There was a lawful secession of Nagorno-Karabakh from Azerbaijan — exactly under the same laws that Azerbaijan left the former Soviet Union. And then there was an attempt forcibly to coerce Karabakh to remain part of Azerbaijan. That's the basis of the conflict...But our goal is independence from Azerbaijan. It's clearly formulated in all our documents...We don't exclude the possibility of a temporary status (of independence) for a transitional period...The more independence, the better." "Karabakhskaya Drama," *op. cit.*

[382]Interview, New York, March 1994.

[383] Liana Minasyan, "Nagorno Karabakh: Nastupleniye armyanskikh formirovanii," *Nezavisimaya Gazeta*, Moscow, April 6, 1993, p. 3.
There has been no outside confirmation of such an Azeri attack in March 1993 against Mardakert and Lachin. Azeri forces periodically shelled the Lachin corridor, the six-mile strip of Azerbaijan separating Armenia from Nagorno Karabakh, but it remained in Armenian hands since its seizure in June 1992 for use as a land resupply route between Armenia and Nagorno-Karabakh.

[384]The Geranboi (Shaumyan) region of Azerbaijan, an area northeast of Karabakh populated in part by Armenians, voted in Karabakh's December 1991 referendum to secede from Azerbaijan.

According to Foreign Minister Gukasyan, "Captured territory is also an object of the negotiations. We don't have any claims to the territory in Azerbaijan and are prepared to view this question in the context of all the rest. . ." In February 1994, Defense Committee Chairman Kocharian commented that, "Each side could now benefit from negotiations: Azerbaijan could get territory and we could get the recognition of the status of the NKR."[385]

The Karabakh Armenians, however, seem unwilling to return certain territories, like Lachin or Kelbajar provinces, and might demand a special status for them. Lachin and Kelbajar form the band of Azerbaijani territory that separates Karabakh from Armenia on the west. At its narrowest part, the city of Lachin, only about ten kilometers separate NKAO from Armenia. Defense Chairman Kocharian has stated that, "Concerning the question, 'All or not all of the (captured) territory', then the Lachin corridor or the Lachin region should be the subject of special discussion during the negotiations. Lachin is the only connection linking us with the outside world. . . . Kelbajar also has a special status and we shouldn't consider conditions for its return to be the same for the return of Agdam or Fizuli."

REPUBLIC OF ARMENIA

The Republic of Armenia insists that it is not party to the conflict and that Azerbaijan must negotiate directly with the Karabakh Armenians.[386]

Very close ties exist between the Republic of Armenia and Nagorno-Karabakh. The Karabakh movement began both in Armenia and in Nagorno-Karabakh, and the present Armenian President Ter-Petrosyan was a member of Armenia's "Karabakh Committee." In July 1992, the Armenian Parliament decreed that it would not sign any international agreement stipulating that Karabakh remained part of Azerbaijan.[387] On June 29, 1992, in a speech before the nation, President Ter-Petrosyan counselled against recognizing the independence of Nagorno-Karabakh in spite of strong parliamentary opposition.[388]

The Armenian Government provides most of the budget to Nagorno-Karabakh — possibly as much as 90 percent — in interest-free credits. Some estimate

---

[385]*Golos Armenii*, Yerevan, February 1, 1994.

[386]Armenia states that it is an "interested party."

[387]Carol Migdalovitz, "Armenia-Azerbaijan Conflict," *CRS Issue Brief*, January 5, 1994, pp. 8-9. Migdalovitz also points out that the December 1, 1989 resolution by the Supreme Soviet of Armenia has not be rescinded.

[388]Schmemann, July 8, 1992, p.3.

that 7 to 9 percent of Armenia's budget goes to support the Karabakh Armenians.[389] The Armenian "Dram" is legal tender in Karabakh, and in August 1994 Armenian Central Bank executives and representatives from Nagorno-Karabakh signed an agreement on monetary union.[390]

The Republic of Armenia provides large-scale humanitarian assistance and fuel to Nagorno-Karabakh, but denies supplying troops or military equipment to Nagorno-Karabakh. In August 1993, however, the Armenian government named Serzhik Sarkissian, the Karabakh defense minister, as defense minister of Armenia.[391] Seiran Baghdasarian, chairman of the Special Commission on Karabakh in the Karabakh Armenian Parliament, told Human Rights Watch/Helsinki that possibly one-sixth of Armenia's population had relatives in Karabakh and thus would often volunteer to fight there.[392] He estimated that Armenian citizens may have numbered 20 percent of the Karabakh Armenian forces during times of full mobilization. At a February 10, 1994, press conference in London, for the first time Armenian President Levon Ter-Petrosyan threatened that Armenia would militarily intervene in Karabakh if genocide or forced deportations faced Armenians living there: "Our people will never allow another genocide to happen."[393] In an April 1994 interview with Human Rights Watch/Helsinki, former Armenian Deputy Foreign Minister Gerard Libaridyan reiterated Armenian military support for Karabakh in case of "forced deportation or genocide."[394]

Armenia has supported an international, negotiated settlement — the Minsk Group talks — both to the fighting and to the ultimate status of Karabakh. Armenia did not recognize the independence of the self-proclaimed Republic of Nagorno-Karabakh. In his speech before the U.N. General Assembly in 1993, Armenian Foreign Minister Papazyan said,

---

[389]Interview, Western diplomat, Yerevan, Armenia. April 1994.

[390]RFE/RL Daily Report, August 31, 1994.

[391]Liana Minasyan, "New Defense Minister Appointed: 'Karabakh Factor in Government Policy," *Nezavisimaya Gazeta*, Moscow, August 24, 1993, p.3., in FBIS-SOV-93-163, August 25, 1993, p. 48.

[392]Interview, Yerevan, Armenia, April 19, 1994. He stated that the number of such volunteers increased greatly in December 1993, after Baghdasarian and other politicians appealed to the populace to support the Karabakh Armenians and volunteer for their cause after the start of an Azerbaijani offensive that lasted from December 1993 to February 1994.

[393]AZG, February 11,1994, in "Daily News Report from Armenia: Armenian Assembly of America," February 11, 1994.

[394]Interview, Yerevan, Armenia, April 19, 1994.

Armenia's position on the Nagorno-Karabakh conflict has been clear and consistent since day one. The conflict is between the people of Nagorno-Karabakh, who are striving for their self-determination, and the Azerbaijani government, which is refusing to address the rights and security concerns of the people of Nagorno-Karabakh. . . . The Government of Armenia sees no alternative to the peaceful settlement of the Karabakh conflict, which can be reached within the framework of the OSCE Minsk Conference.[395]

According to Libaridyan, the Armenian position consists of the following phases: cease-fire and separation of forces by third party forces, negotiations to work towards the removal of blockades against Armenia, withdrawal of Karabakh forces from Azerbaijan, and settlement of Karabakh's political status.[396]

The Armenian Government welcomed Russian efforts to end the conflict, but has been wary of Turkish ceasefire efforts or of peace plans that include Turkish military participation. It also rejects Turkish peacekeepers in any buffer force between Karabakh and Azerbaijani forces.

[395]Address of Armenian Foreign Minister Vahan Papazyan to the United Nations General Assembly, October 1993.

[396]Interview, Yerevan, April 20, 1994.

APPENDIX C: LETTERS TO/FROM PRESIDENT LEVON TER-PETROSYAN

HUMAN RIGHTS WATCH/HELSINKI
Formerly Helsinki Watch

■ 485 Fifth Avenue, New York, NY 10017-6104, TEL (212) 972-8400, FAX (212) 972-0905, Email: hrwatchnyc@igc.apc.org
❏ 1522 K Street, NW, #910, Washington, DC 20005-1202, TEL (202) 371-6592, FAX (202) 371-0124, Email: hrwatchdc@igc.apc.org
❏ 90 Borough High Street, London, UK SE1 1LL, TEL (71) 378-8008, FAX (71) 378-8029, Email: hrwatchuk@gn.apc.org
❏ Moscow, Russian Federation, TEL and FAX (7095) 265-4448

JERI LABER
Executive Director
LOIS WHITMAN
Deputy Director
HOLLY CARTNER
JULIE MERTUS
Counsels
ERIKA DAILEY
RACHEL DENBER
IVANA NIZICH
CHRISTOPHER PANICO
Research Associates

Advisory Committee
Jonathan Fanton, Chair
Alice H. Henkin, Vice Chair
Roland Algrant
Robert L. Bernstein
Charles Biblowit
Martin Blumenthal
Roberta Cohen
Lori Damrosch
Istvan Deak
Adrian W. DeWind
Fr. Robert Drinan
Stanley Engelstein
Alan R. Finberg
Ellen Futter
Willard Gaylin, MD
Michael Gellert
John Glusman
Paul Goble
Robert K. Goldman
Jack Greenberg
Rita E. Hauser
Robert James
Rhoda Karpatkin
Stephen L. Kass
Bentley Kassal
Marina Pinto Kaufman
Joanne Landy
Margaret A. Lang
Leon Levy
Wendy Luers
Theodor Meron
Deborah Milenkovitch
Toni Morrison
John B. Oakes
Herbert Okun
Jane Olson
Yuri Orlov
Srdja Popovic
Bruce Rabb
Peter Reddaway
Stuart Robinowitz
John G. Ryden
Herman Schwartz
Stanley K. Sheinbaum
Jerome J. Shestack
George Soros
Susan Weber Soros
Michael Sovern
Fritz Stern
Svetlana Stone
Rose Styron
Liv Ullman
Gregory Wallance
Rosalind Whitehead
Jerome R. Wiesner
William D. Zabel

March 2, 1994

President Levon Ter-Petrossian
Marshal Bagramian Prospect, 26
375019 Yerevan

By Fax: 52-15-81

Dear President Ter-Petrossian,

Human Rights/Helsinki (formerly Helsinki Watch) is the largest human rights organization in the United States. We have closely followed the war in Nagorno Karabakh, and have published two reports on violations of the Geneva Conventions in that conflict.

I am writing you today to express our organization's deep concern about the deaths of Azerbaijani prisoners of war in Armenia. According to the International Committee of the Red Cross, the following men were shot to death in an Armenian detention camp in Spitak in late January or early February:

Rustam Ramazan-ogly Agaev, (birthdate unknown), from Masalin District
Elman Mamed-ogly Akhmedov, b. 1961, from Yevlakh District
Elshan Hussein-ogly Akhmedov, b. 1974, from Saatlin District
Bakhram Akif-ogly Giiasov, b. 1972, from Siazan
Faig Gabil-ogly Guliev, b. 1969, from Baku
Enver Asker-ogly Jafarov, b. 1972, from Sumgait
Eldar Sakhbaba-ogly Mamedov, b. 1966, from Baku
Girshad Kniaz-ogly Mamedov, b. 1974, from Yevlakh

The Armenian Ministry of Foreign Affairs claims that the prisoners were shot while attempting to escape. In accordance with the Geneva Convention Relative to the Treatment of Prisoners of War, articles 89 and 92, attempts to escape from detention may be punished only by disciplinary sanctions. We are aware of the Ministry of Defense's claim that the shooting was the result of a fight that broke out among the prisoners attempting to escape. Because this version does not fully correspond to that of the Ministry of Foreign Affairs, we look upon it with skepticism. We

HUMAN RIGHTS WATCH   KENNETH ROTH, Executive Director · CYNTHIA BROWN, Program Director · HOLLY J. BURKHALTER, Advocacy Director · GARA LaMARCHE, Associate Director · JUAN E. MÉNDEZ, General Counsel · SUSAN OSNOS, Communications Director · ROBERT L. BERNSTEIN, Chair · ADRIAN W. DeWIND, Vice Chair
Human Rights Watch is a not-for-profit corporation monitoring and promoting human rights in Africa, the Americas, Asia, the Middle East, and among the signatories of the Helsinki accords

President Ter-Petrossian
March 2, 1994
Page Two

urge you to use your good offices to ensure that the investigation of this incident is thorough and objective, that it includes competent international organizations willing to participate, that its results are made public as quickly as possible, and that the guilty parties are punished.

Human Rights Watch\Helsinki takes no sides in the war in Nagorno Karabakh. We are equally concerned about Azerbaijani prisoners of war detained in Armenia and Nagorno Karabakh as we are about their Armenian counterparts in Azerbaijan.

I thank you for your attention to this matter and look forward to learning the results of the investigation.

Yours sincerely,

Jeri Laber
Executive Director

HUMAN RIGHTS WATCH/HELSINKI

Formerly Helsinki Watch

■ 485 Fifth Avenue, New York, NY 10017-6104, TEL (212) 972-8400, FAX (212) 972-0905, Email: hrwatchnyc@igc.apc.org
❏ 1522 K Street, NW, #910, Washington, DC 20005-1202, TEL (202) 371-6592, FAX (202) 371-0124, Email: hrwatchdc@igc.apc.org
❏ 90 Borough High Street, London, UK SE1 1LL, TEL (71) 378-8008, FAX (71) 378-8029, Email: hrwatchuk@gn.apc.org
❏ Moscow, Russian Federation, TEL and FAX (7095) 265-4448

JERI LABER
Executive Director
LOIS WHITMAN
Deputy Director
HOLLY CARTNER
JULIE MERTUS
Counsels
ERIKA DAILEY
RACHEL DENBER
IVANA NIZICH
CHRISTOPHER PANICO
Research Associates

Advisory Committee
Jonathan Fanton, Chair
Alice H. Henkin, Vice Chair
Roland Algrant
Robert L. Bernstein
Charles Biblowit
Martin Blumenthal
Roberta Cohen
Lori Damrosch
Istvan Deak
Adrian W. DeWind
Fr. Robert Drinan
Stanley Engelstein
Alan R. Finberg
Ellen Futter
Willard Gaylin, MD
Michael Gellert
John Glusman
Paul Goble
Robert K. Goldman
Jack Greenberg
Rita E. Hauser
Robert James
Rhoda Karpatkin
Stephen L. Kass
Bentley Kassal
Marina Pinto Kaufman
Joanne Landy
Margaret A. Lang
Leon Levy
Wendy Luers
Theodor Meron
Deborah Milenkovitch
Toni Morrison
John B. Oakes
Herbert Okun
Jane Olson
Yuri Orlov
Srdja Popovic
Bruce Rabb
Peter Reddaway
Stuart Robinowitz
John G. Ryden
Herman Schwartz
Stanley K. Sheinbaum
Jerome J. Shestack
George Soros
Susan Weber Soros
Michael Sovern
Fritz Stern
Svetlana Stone
Rose Styron
Liv Ullman
Gregory Wallance
Rosalind Whitehead
Jerome R. Wiesner
William D. Zabel

May 2, 1994

President Levon Ter-Petrossian
Marshal Bagramian Prospect, 26
375019 Yerevan

By Fax: 52-15-81

Dear Mr. President:

On March 2, I wrote you on behalf of Human Rights Watch/Helsinki, expressing concern at the deaths of eight Azerbaijan prisoners on January 29, 1994. The prisoners were in the custody of the Armenian Ministry of Defense. As you know, the prisoners are alleged to have died during an escape attempt after the murder of one prison guard. In my letter of March 2, I called on you to ensure a fair and unbiased investigation of the incident, which would include competent international organizations. Several facts regarding the events of January 29, 1994, recently brought to my attention force me to repeat my call for a complete and impartial inquiry with international participation into the deaths of the eight Azeri prisoners.

On April 4, Human Rights Watch/Helsinki staff members in Azerbaijan spoke with Dr. Rafik Yusifli, Chairman of the Scientific Society of Forensic Medicine of Azerbaijan and head of the medical team that performed autopsies on the eight prisoners. Doctor Yusifli stated that six of the men died of close range bullet wounds to the head, one was shot through the chest, and one had his throat slit. Dr. Derrik Pounder of Scotland's University of Dundee Department of Forensic Medicine travelled to Azerbaijan and confirmed Dr. Yusufli's findings regarding the cause of death of the eight men. Dr. Pounder stated that "the pattern of injuries of the six individuals who died of gunshot wounds to the head suggest mass execution, but the possibility of a mass suicide cannot be absolutely excluded."

On April 20, in a discussion with Human Rights Watch/Helsinki staff members visiting Armenia, the Military Procurator of Armenia who is conducting the investigation, Vagarshak Vardanian, stated that the eight prisoners died within minutes after killing a guard and seizing his pistol and sixteen rounds of ammunition (two magazines of eight rounds each). According to Mr. Vardanian, the prisoners decided to commit suicide after they realized their escape attempt was doomed. Mr. Vardanian stated that seven of the men died from wounds received from one pistol within several minutes. Mr. Vardanian also stated that other prisoners who witnessed the escape and subsequent deaths of the men

HUMAN KENNETH ROTH, Executive Director · CYNTHIA BROWN, Program Director · HOLLY J. BURKHALTER, Advocacy Director
RIGHTS GARA LAMARCHE, Associate Director · JUAN E. MÉNDEZ, General Counsel · SUSAN OSNOS, Communications Director
WATCH   ROBERT L. BERNSTEIN, Chair · ADRIAN W. DeWIND, Vice Chair
        Human Rights Watch is a not for profit corporation monitoring and promoting human rights in Africa, the Americas, Asia, the Middle East, and among the signatories of the Helsinki accords

corroborate his version. The Bureau of Forensic Medicine of the Armenian Ministry of Health has conducted autopsies on the bodies and returned them to Azerbaijan, but, according to Mr. Vardanian, has yet to release its results.

While the result of the Armenian government inquiry into the deaths has not yet been released, Mr. Vardanian's account of seven men committing suicide with one pistol in the space of several minutes raises considerable doubt. First, it contradicts earlier official versions of the event. Shortly after the incident, the Armenian Ministry of Foreign Affairs stated that the men died during an escape attempt, while according to the Azerbaijani government the Armenian Ministry of Defense claimed that the prisoners died as a result of a fight among them. Also, the fact that the military procurator is conducting an investigation of an event that occurred in a prison subordinate to the Ministry of Defense casts further doubt on the impartiality of the investigation. Finally, Mr. Vardanian stated that other prisoners witnessed the event and corroborate his account. Eight of these men, however, are presently on trial for hostage-taking and murder, five on capital charges. Thus their statements, while possibly truthful, lose credibility in the face of their predicament.

I respectfully urge you to open up the investigation to include competent international organizations. Only through their participation will the investigation put an end to the unfortunate incident of January 29, 1994.

I thank you for your attention to this matter and eagerly await the results of the investigation.

Respectfully,

Jeri Laber
Jeri Laber
Executive Director

REPUBLIC OF ARMENIA   **OFFICE OF THE PRESIDENT**

Jeri Laber
Executive Director
Human Rights Watch
485 5th Avenue
New York, NY 10017-6104
United States

August 15, 1994

Dear Ms. Laber,

In response to your letter of May 2, 1994, President Ter-Petrossian has asked me to communicate the following:

No executions have taken place in Armenia during President Levon Ter-Petrossian's term in office. Further, I can assure you that this policy will not be changed during the remainder of his tenure.

I would like, further, to convey the following information: Bakhtian Khanali ogly Shabiev and Garai Muzafar ogly Nagiev were sentenced to death by the Supreme Court of Armenia on April 5, 1994 for their murder of three Armenian civilians in the Martuni District of Armenia and their attempt to poison a water reservoir.

The penalty of death was handed out in accordance with Sections 4 and 8 of Article 99 of the Criminal Code of the Republic of Armenia which deal with the "murder of two or more persons." The two accused were tried under the Criminal Code as common criminals and do not qualify as prisoners of war. Their action outside of the area of military operations, their arrest on Armenian territory and the strictly criminal nature of their attack explains their treatment as common criminals.

May I add that the President is ready to give serious consideration to any appeal for the commuting of their sentences if an appeal is made by the two individuals in question.

Gerard Libaridian
Advisor to the President